for *The Ups*

MW01680980

"*The Upside of Falling* is more than a book—it's a deep exhale for the creative soul. Kephart reminds us that surrender is not defeat but the doorway to freedom. Every page rekindles the courage to write from the heart."

— Marni Freedman, author of *Artistic Badassery* and founder of the San Diego Writers Festival

"What Kephart has done here is trailblazing! She guides us to free our writer's soul and shows us that letting go of fear has an upside—much like falling in love. *The Upside of Falling* is a treasure map guiding us back to our own source of inspiration."

— Marijke McCandless, mindfulness coach and award-winning author of *Naked in the Now*

"Kephart crafts a lifeline for writers to turn vulnerability into strength. Embrace the fall."

— Laura "Mercy Hollow" Perkins, author, editor, CEO of DarkDD Media

"Cherie edits with compassion and honesty. She motivates and challenges, which results in better poems, essays, stories, and books. I am honored to have her edit my work."

— Leslie Ferguson, award-winning author of *When I Was Her Daughter*

"Cherie helped me polish my novel into its best work—and I landed a literary agent who loves it as much as I do."

— Kirk Rafferty, author of *Cosmonaut and the Fisherman*

"Cherie tunes into the heart of the message you want to share and brings it out beautifully. Her keen editorial talents help you convey your inspired message in a clear and impactful way."

— Suresh Ramaswamy, award-winning author of *Just Be*

"Cherie Kephart has taken the lessons from her popular classes and expanded them into a guide for nurturing the writer's soul. A valuable resource for writers and creatives ready to reinvigorate their process."

— Mary Vensel White, author, editor, and publisher

"Cherie's suggestions were clear and capable, and her supportive demeanor got me to the finish line. Her professionalism and encouragement were exactly what I needed to complete my book."

— Teri Roche Drobnick, author of *Moving Day* and *Our Long Goodbye*

"Cherie's insights didn't just polish my poetry, they elevated it. I grew as a writer and now see my work in new ways."

— Swamini Brahmanishtananda, poet and author of *I'm Not My Story*

"If you're ready to dig deep and create lasting characters readers love, hire Cherie. You will thank yourself (and Cherie) when the royalty checks come in."

—Jamie Della, author of *A Box of Magick*

"Working with Cherie was the best thing that could have happened to my book. With her big-picture insight and precise edits, my manuscript transformed into something I'm proud to share."

—Jonathan Gillard Daly, actor and author of *Rough Magic*

"I now have a compelling manuscript thanks to Cherie's expert feedback. She is the best of the best."

— Diáne Mandle, award-winning author of *Ancient Sounds for a New Age*

"Cherie Kephart is a master conductor in the world of writing and editing. Her feedback is sage, specific, and dedicated to creating an overall harmonious piece of writing."

— Ravi Sahay, author of *My Health Is Your Wealth*

"From the first moments of working with Cherie, I knew she understood what I was trying to accomplish with my book. Even when I resisted suggestions at first, I soon realized she was right—her feedback always made my book stronger and more impactful for readers."

— Shannon Duncan, author of *Present Moment Awareness* and *Coming Full Circle*

"Cherie is the gold standard when it comes to coaching and editing. Authentic, supportive, and brilliant in her insight."

— Dusty Thompson, author of *Prison Stripes and Penny Loafers*

"Meeting and working with Cherie Kephart has been an absolute game changer. She customizes her coaching to each client's needs and is the perfect balance of professional and personal."

— Laura Orrantia, children's book author

"My writing has grown so much since I began coaching sessions with Cherie. During my most recent meeting with her, I got chills because the connections she was helping me make about my book were exactly what I needed. I look forward to working with Cherie for years to come!"

— Sarah Maloy Bailey, freelance editor, author, and poet

THE UPSIDE OF FALLING

THE UPSIDE OF FALLING

CONNECTING TO THE ART AND HEART OF BEING A WRITER

CHERIE KEPHART

BAZI PUBLISHING

BAZI
PUBLISHING

Bazi Publishing
San Diego, California
BaziPublishing.com

For more information, email cherie@cheriekephart.com or visit BaziPublishing.com.

Publisher's Congress Cataloging-in-Publication Data

Names: Kephart, Cherie, author.

Title: The upside of falling : connecting to the art and heart of being a writer / Cherie Kephart.

Description: San Diego, California : Bazi Publishing, [2026]

Identifiers: LCCN: 2025921478 | ISBN: 9781947127135 (paperback) | 9781947127159 (ebook) | 9781947127166 (audiobook)

Subjects: LCSH: Authorship--Psychological aspects. | Creative ability. | Creative thinking. | Inspiration. | Self-realization. | Self-confidence. | Self-actualization (Psychology) | LCGFT: Self-help publications. | BISAC: SELF-HELP / Creativity. | LANGUAGE ARTS & DISCIPLINES / Writing / General. | SELF-HELP / Motivational & Inspirational.

Classification: LCC: PN171.P83 K46 2026 | DDC: 808.02/019--dc23

Printed in the United States of America
10 9 8 7 6 5 4 3 2 1

Book jacket and page design: Asa Wild of WildGraphics
Author photograph: Ariana Cohen

for you as you fall

CONTENTS

fall•ing
verb

1. coming down freely under the influence of gravity
2. passing into a new state of body, mind, or situation

First, we are open. Then, everything flows.

INVITATION

This is not a book about the craft of writing.

Now hear me out.

The comedian Kevin Nealon once did a bit on that phrase, "Now hear me out." The premise was that nothing good ever comes after those words. Think about it. "I'm going to lower you into the well by your ankles. Now hear me out." I laughed so hard at this I almost peed my pants.

Since that day, I've thought a lot about this phrase. It asks us to listen, to be open, to broaden our view about something—something new, unusual, or even outlandish. Mostly, it is an invitation to expand our awareness and shift our perspective.

This book is not about the skills, techniques, and tools of writing. It's not about how to work harder to accomplish writing goals. And it's certainly not about the proper use of the often-misunderstood semicolon.

Instead, this book is about you.

This book is an invitation to trust, let go, and discover the deeper aspects of who you are as a writer. It's also about freeing yourself so you can create in the most joyous and liberating way possible. Writing is determined by the relationship we have with ourselves—how we show up and what is happening inside us. When we cultivate a greater understanding of our inner terrain and unravel the hidden layers holding us back, we enter the unwritten, a magical place beyond words.

We transform.

One of my favorite quotes is by Tibetan Buddhist meditation master Chögyam Trungpa: "The bad news is you're falling through the air, nothing to hang on to, no parachute. The good news is, there's no ground."

The Upside of Falling is about gaining a new perspective. We may be plummeting and feeling like we are out of control—which we are. Yet, we can shift our vantage point and feel the freedom that comes along with falling. How incredible is it to fall, knowing we won't ever hit ground? That is the art and heart of being a writer, and it all starts within you.

Falling is about being, not forcing or trying to make it something other than it is. You are falling. Period. So, fall. Yes, it can feel scary. Let go of whatever it is you are trying to hold on to. Both hands free.

The best part is you are not alone. About a gazillion and a half other writers are falling, too. Together, we will venture into Falling 101. The first thing to remember is this: Don't look down. Keep your gaze uplifted to the wonder of it all. Embrace who you are, accept what is, and enjoy the fall.

PART ONE
Inspiration

To inspire and bring joy to others, we first need to inspire and bring joy to ourselves.

CHAPTER ONE

Be Present

There are two kinds of writers. Those who want to *write* and those who want to *have written*.

Many people want to write a book to say they *have written* a book, or they want to use the book for some other reason. They don't actually want to *write* it. They are focused on getting to the end. They deem the writing process to be something they must endure and don't recognize it for what it really is—magic.

Writing is being in a flow, being fully present. You are immersed in a creative endeavor. Yes, there are benefits at the end, but you wouldn't want to skip the process. You would miss the magic.

Imagine a favorite activity besides writing. I'll choose playing tennis. I want to *play* tennis, not come home at the end of the day and just *say*, "I played tennis." Or eating a pomegranate. I want to delight in the crisp, tart flavor on my tongue, not tell people, "Hey, I ate a pomegranate."

The present moment is here. In it, there is always something beneficial and pleasing. Connect with that. Relish the process. Don't miss the magic.

Being fully present is also about releasing resistance. I know, much easier said than done. But it's hard to enjoy the fall with a bunch of things producing friction. We need to take a closer look at the barriers keeping us from fully embracing the fall. We can even let go of the identity we attribute to being a writer. Yes, I use the term "writer" as a tool for communication. And yes, we are writers. It's beautiful. However, that identity is not who we really are. At our essence, we are creative beings. Beings with infinite potential and possibilities. When we let go of the concept of *writer* and embrace the *being* part, we are more in tune with our experience crafting words. How do we do this? That's the innovative piece.

The more relaxed, aware, and willing we are to just be with our words, the less we feel like we are trying and the more we feel like we are in the joy of the moment. Then, there is less and less resistance. We change from always doing and striving to simply being with what unfolds. We begin to enjoy the fall, and our creations are then fueled from a passionate and inspired space within us.

We writers often get in our own way. Not only do we try so hard, push, cajole, and aim for results all the time, but we also often ignore our inspiration and do not fully value the time spent in creation. We many times want to rush to the end. But an innovative endeavor is not about the result or product but the path you take. It is not about your label as a "writer" but you, *the being*, having the experience with your words in the moment. After all, this present moment is all there is.

What can happen in the future can be important. It can be big. The outcome can be rewarding and magnificent, giving us incentives to keep going. But there is nothing to be gained by focusing on those results now. Stay in the moment.

Sometimes worry can seep in. That's common. We writers tend to concern ourselves with all sorts of things that never come true. Worry doesn't help anyone or anything. It actually impedes our freedom to create. Letting go of our worries is not easy. Worry feels like a natural part of being human. By noticing our worries and how they distract us from the present, we can start turning our awareness to them and focus on letting them go, one by one. This can take time. The first step is to simply notice, then to acknowledge what is troubling you. Then, you can redirect your attention to more positive and constructive thoughts. Thoughts that serve you.

Making a concerted choice to focus on what is being created now—whether it's the first draft or you're deep into the revision process—is the most important thing you can do. Bring yourself back into awareness to experience the moment in front of you. The more present and connected you are, the more powerful that moment and your writing will be.

It is often said that a good writer is one who writes. Indeed. However, since good and bad are subjective, let's strip away those qualifications. For you, the joy of being a writer may be in thinking about writing and enjoying the idea of writing. Or it may be writing once a day or week, no matter how many funny cat videos or bingeworthy shows are dangled before you. For me, the joy is derived from the emotional connection I experience each time I write, cherishing wherever it takes me.

Try letting go of the label of writer and the idea of being a "good" writer. This is a big part of the fall. Be whatever it is that brings you joy. Be present in the moment as you string words together. Let the experience illuminate that part of you waiting to be awakened. Be 100% in the moment, falling and feeling the wind on your face.

You may wonder how I arrived at all this falling stuff. I have decades of experience with falling, but there was one event that solidified it all for me. It's what I call my "ambulance moment."

At thirty-two years old, I collapsed in my shower. Wet and naked, I crawled to the phone and called for help. I was taken to the emergency room that night, which was the start of seven years spent searching for answers to a mysterious illness. I had two goals: (1) find a diagnosis and (2) try not to die. I thought they were good goals.

I had more than twenty debilitating symptoms that left me bedridden, hallucinating, and being spoon-fed to stay alive. I visited doctor after doctor; no one had any answers. I was dying and I didn't even know why.

I felt mountains of fear. Once a successful technical writer, avid runner and beach volleyball player, and world traveler to more than forty countries, I was afraid and unable to leave my house.

Until one day, I was in the back of an ambulance being rushed to the hospital, my heart rate up to 185 beats per minute. A paramedic leaned over me and said, "You're going to be okay."

In that moment, I thought about all my years of suffering and how I was so afraid of death that I was no longer living. I'd been constantly fearful and worried and resisting everything that was happening to me.

I was no longer present.

As the sirens blared and an IV was thrust into my arm, I saw my fear. It was a dark shroud extinguishing my light. I thought, What if I just stopped being scared? What if I took a chance and released my fear? How would it feel? I figured I could always go back to the fear; it would still be there. I had nothing to lose since I was already dying.

I tried it.

My body and mind instantly relaxed. The overall feeling was euphoric—and it wasn't whatever they put in my IV. I looked up at the paramedic and said, "You're right. Even if I die, I'm going to be okay." With that realization, I felt free.

This wasn't an easy feat. It took years for me to understand the power I had within me to change my perspective, to shift my whole experience. But once I did, the resistance that had been keeping me imprisoned vanished.

In this life, we all fall, and we all experience fear. But we have a choice. How we handle the fall and the fear—that makes all the difference.

My fear always felt like I was falling, with nothing to hang on to and the ground quickly approaching. That day in the ambulance, I felt what that Zen monk said—there is no ground. There is merely the freedom of being.

The point is this: When we are writing, we want to tap into the present moment. The present holds our joy and passion, our strength of creation, and it's where the beauty happens.

Being present isn't just some new age idea to try to calm our minds and bring more peace into our hearts (although it does). When we are present, we embrace the power we have within ourselves to transform our lives. No one else can do it for us.

Present moment awareness is a gift. It helps us shed everything that keeps us from engaging with the beauty in our lives, even those deep, dark moments. Especially those moments, because often the darkest parts of our lives turn out to be the most meaningful.

Find that place in you that yearns to be here and now with your words. Give yourself over fully to those moments of creation. You will feel the difference that presence brings to your writing. You will feel the magic.

Practice & Play

At the end of each chapter, I have provided practices to inspire you, spark your imagination, nurture your inner writer, and help you with the creation process. Some practices you'll use over and over, and others maybe only once. I encourage you to read the whole book through first, and then you can go back and decide which practices you want to try.

Here are some simple yet powerful practices to support you on your quest to become more present and connected with your writing process.

WARM UP

To keep our awareness in the moment as we write, we need to let go of distractions, worries, and thoughts of other aspects of our life. This is your time to write. There is only you and the keyboard, or the pen, as your heart and mind flow together to create a one-of-a-kind collection of words. By staying present, your words will be more authentic, relatable, and powerful for you and for the reader. You can tell if you are present because you will feel an enhanced focus and be more connected to what you are doing. You will feel more relaxed and available to your writing.

Spend five minutes freewriting before your intended writing session. It's like stretching before you exercise. This will release the frenetic energy from the day's tasks and anything else you have on your mind, so you can focus on your story. Set a timer, grab a pen and paper, and write anything and everything that wants to come out. Do not edit, censor, or force anything. Let whatever wants to be written come. This will help you transition from the outside world of doing to the inside world of being.

CONNECT WITH YOUR BREATH

Connecting with our breath is one of the most important things we can do as a writer. Our breath is our life force, where all creativity comes from. Deep, fluid breaths help relax our nervous system and thereby open us to fully connecting to the present moment, which frees our imagination. Before you write, place your hand on your belly and notice your breath. Are you breathing fast? Have you been holding your breath? Don't try to change your breath, but merely notice it for a few seconds. You don't need to do anything. By bringing your attention to your breath, it will naturally slow down and transport you into the now. During your writing sessions, set a timer for every fifteen or thirty minutes, reminding you to check your breath. The more you get used to checking your breath and breathing deeper, the more natural it will feel and the more at ease you'll be when you write.

CHECK IN

Before you write, you can check in with yourself by taking a little time to see where your attention is. Find a quiet space where you can reflect and answer the following inquiries. Write about whatever comes up, without overthinking. The key is to be gentle with yourself. Honor what comes up. Know that wherever you are is exactly where you need to be. Then, after you've answered these questions, simply be with what came up. Awareness is a beautiful step to freeing us as we fall.

- What is holding me back from being fully present right now in this moment?

- What do I need in order to be focused and free of distractions for this writing session?

TAKE ONE MINUTE TO WRITE

We have full lives with families, relationships, jobs, homes, responsibilities, and self-care needs. It can feel challenging to find time to write. Although we all have the same twenty-four hours in a day, not everyone has the same availability. But we can all find one minute a day. One minute may not sound like enough to accomplish anything, but dedicating one minute a day does a few things. First, it creates a habit. You are declaring to the world that you will make time for writing. Second, it creates space for you to write. Every day, you get this one minute. Third, when you sit to write for one minute, most of the time you won't stop at just one minute. Once you get into the flow, you'll want to keep going. Last, writing is cumulative. It doesn't happen all in one writing session (okay, sometimes a shorter piece will, but even that requires revisions and editing). A little bit each day adds up, and one day you'll look back and see how much writing you've done. Most importantly, you'll notice how much more present you've become, which will in turn enhance your craft.

CHAPTER TWO

Be Clear

If this present moment is all there is—since the past has vanished, and we don't know yet about the future—then how we spend our *now* becomes our life. Why, then, do we spend so much of it writing? That's a great question.

Recently, I taught a workshop at a writers' conference. It was about the spirit and being of writing. It's the most emotionally charged workshop I teach. Over the years of attending and being part of the staff at these conferences, I've seen so many incredible workshops and books about writing, but my favorites are those that focus not on the writing per se, but on the writer.

During my workshop, one guy in a light-blue flannel shirt and jeans was sitting in the back corner of the room all by himself. I had seen him before, but we run in different writing circles, and, to my knowledge, he had never taken any of my workshops. His genre of choice—dystopian fiction.

After thirty minutes, he got up and left. I paid no attention and kept going. At the end of the conference weekend, he came up to me with a light in his eyes and said, "I want to thank you."

A warmth of energy cradled my heart. "What for?"

Tears formed in his eyes. "In those thirty minutes in your workshop, I found what I've been searching for."

For five years, he had yearned for an answer, and what I offered in my class helped him find it. Now I started to cry. We both laughed and felt connected to something bigger than writing.

What did he find in those thirty minutes? His *why*.

He held a lot of anger about his life, and without realizing it, he was compelled to write to this darkness festering inside him. But until my class, he never connected the dots. Never understood the fodder for his fury. With this new insight, he felt unburdened.

Clarity is an essential aspect of writing. If readers can't understand what we are saying and what we mean, there is no resonance with our words. The type of clarity I want to focus on is even grander than that; it's being clear about why you are writing.

Why do you write? Why are you writing that particular piece? That book? That article? That poem? That song? You could be writing about anything. Why that?

Do you know?

If you don't know why you are writing, your readers will sense that you don't. If you don't have a clear idea of why you want to write, it will be hard to be present and stay motivated. If you don't understand the bigger picture of your life and why writing is important to you, anything you write will be flat or lack flow. You could end up like the guy in the workshop who struggled for years, not understanding why he carried so much pain and anger while writing unsatisfying dark dystopian novels until he was willing to ask himself the hard questions.

When we are not in alignment with our why, we can get off course, stunt our growth, and block our creativity. We live in a place of struggle and suffering. We reside in the dark. To change this, we need to open ourselves up and dig deep because with clarity comes freedom.

Let's go deeper into the why. I've identified some common reasons we write and put them into two categories. Let's look at the first one.

WHY PITFALLS

- Become famous
- Become rich
- Expose the truth
- Feel good enough
- Feel loved
- Gain accomplishments
- Gain approval
- Get recognition
- Get revenge
- Increase social status
- Prove something
- Receive praise
- Win awards

These *why* pitfalls all have an energy that is about needing, searching, or trying to get something out of the writing, from our readers, or from the world. They are extrinsic motivations, which means they come from external rewards or pressures. You do something to earn a reward or avoid punishment. These motivations are about the surface part of us. Some of these outcomes might happen, but if they are the primary reasons we write, the writing experience and the words may be shallow. People won't connect with your message, your theme, or you. Your words won't reach them on the deepest levels.

These motivations are about the outer experience. They are pitfalls keeping you stuck. Your yearning for outer goals will be like chasing something shiny that doesn't really drive you, ignite you, or bring you to life.

Let's look at the other category.

HARMONIOUS *WHYS*

- Connect with the power of words
- Connect with readers
- Connect with yourself
- Connect with something bigger and more expansive than yourself
- Contribute to the collective works of literature
- Delve into compelling concepts and ideas
- Discover something new
- Embark on an adventure
- Explore your innermost truths
- Express your creativity
- Get lost in the joy of a story or new world
- Give a voice to those who don't have one
- Grow and transform
- Heal from your past
- Help others on their journey
- Hone your craft
- Improve the knowledge and wisdom of a concept, industry, or subject
- Inspire and motivate

- Play and have fun
- Pursue your deepest passion
- Realize a beautiful dream
- Share your hard-earned wisdom with the world
- Share your unique human experience
- Write because you can't imagine doing anything else

Do you feel the difference? All the whys on this second list come from a more expansive, inspired place. They are intrinsic motivations, coming from within. You engage in an activity because you find it personally rewarding, enjoyable, or meaningful. They stem from a sense of purity and joy, not from wanting or needing. They focus on the process, not the result or a product. They focus on purpose, beliefs, and why you get up in the morning and can't wait to start writing. They are full of energy and will contribute something positive to your life and to the collective.

A lovely and talented nonfiction writer was referred to me by a friend for some writing coaching for her self-help book. She was stuck in her writing, stressed, and worried. I listened to her about all the concerns and problems she was facing for the past three years while she had been working on her manuscript. Procrastination. Stress. Worry. Not feeling good enough. And on and on. After a while she paused and asked me what I thought.

I said, "Let me ask you a question. Why are you writing this book?"

"To make some money but also to make sure I am heard. I want people to hear what I have to say, and I want to show them that this is important."

I gave her a moment to be with her why, and then I broke the silence. "What if you spend another year or two and finish this book, it gets published, and no one buys or reads it? How would you feel?"

Her voice was strained. "I would feel awful, like I wasted all those years of my life." She started to cry.

I could feel her sadness. Without knowing, she was caught up in extrinsic motivations. I had been there before, and I know many other artists who have too. I wanted to give her hope. "I'm sure that would feel awful. And I definitely don't want that to happen to you. But we can't control who, if anyone, will buy and read our books. Since there has been nothing in this endeavor for you except the possible outcome, which you can't count on, of course you are going to feel stressed. Everything is riding on what you produce."

Her crying stopped.

I continued. "If you can find a deeper, more meaningful reason you are spending all this time writing, then no matter who reads your book or doesn't, you will never consider it wasted time. The process will be fulfilling, and any results will be a bonus."

So many of us put undue pressure on ourselves. This not only separates us from the joy and presence we gain from writing but also causes us to unknowingly generate suffering.

Let me give you one more example. I was teaching a class and gave everyone an exercise to figure out their why. People shared what they had discovered, and it got emotional (I need to remember to bring some tissues next time). One woman didn't look happy during the entire exercise, so I asked her if she wanted any help.

She said, "I've been working on my memoir for years. I want to share my story and get rid of some of the stigma about my mental health disorder. And I can't seem to finish, and I don't know if I'll ever get it published, and it's depressing."

The class got silent. We could all feel her frustration. I approached her and looked into her eyes. "I hear you. Your feelings are valid. Writing can feel like a long process, like it's never going to end. I know, I've been there. But let me ask you something. If you can look at all these years researching and writing about your life, have you learned or gained any new insights?"

She simply stared at me. Silence. Then tears. (Told you I should have had tissues). She wiped her face on her sleeve. "Yes. I see myself so differently, and I now have self-compassion. I feel like I can forgive myself for everything I've done."

One of the other students chimed in. "Do you think you would have arrived at these insights about yourself if you hadn't written the book?"

She hesitated, then said, "No."

In that moment, the feeling in that room was magical. All of us felt inspired. We learn so much from our fellow writers. This day was certainly no exception.

Within a year of that day, this woman finished writing her book and found a publisher. The best part? She is radiant, no longer beholden to antiquated ideas about who she is or why she wrote her book. Being vulnerable and discovering her why and what the writing gave her have produced freedom and clarity to move forward.

Let me be clear. It is not always simple or easy to change from focusing on extrinsic motivations to embracing intrinsic ones. It can be a process of unwinding beliefs and values and can take time. The main point is to be aware of what is fueling your writing.

And it's not always easy or simple to uncover our why. But it's there. Sometimes we hide it. Sometimes we hide from it.

Maybe you don't know your why right now. That's okay. You may, like this woman, discover it along the way. Just know that your *why* is what's important, not the outcome. And when you learn to trust yourself, it can come into focus. Perhaps just take a guess about your why. Give yourself permission to get it totally wrong. But my bet is that if you try, you'll hit a bullseye. The clearer you are about your why, the more you'll be able to free-fall. And that can be super fun. Who doesn't want more fun?

Practice & Play

Being clear about our process, desires, and passions for our writing will uncover so much for us. It can propel us to greater heights with our words and our life. These practices are designed to get you in touch with your why and become as clear as you can be about the reasons you write. Know that your why can change over time, and per project, as you transform and grow. Come back again and again to these practices for each new stage or project. Or simply for different times in your life. Staying clear will keep you motivated and focused, and it will help keep your writing flowing. If you feel any resistance, that's okay. It's common. Just notice it, and be gentle with yourself. Stay connected to your deepest desires and what lights you up. Give yourself some space and time to do these practices. Some may feel easy while others a little more challenging. Know that you are carving a path for yourself and your writing, one full of possibility and wonder. It's worth the exploration. Any emotions that surface are most likely ready to be felt and released. How freeing is that?

DISCOVER YOUR WHY

Why? is a formidable question. Discovering your why can take time. Not the superficial why but the truest reason you write. Go there and you will be rewarded. Take some quiet time to answer these inquiries from the most honest and open place you can.

- Why do I write?
- Why am I writing this story?

- Why is it important to me?
- Why do I want to finish this book/project?

MAKE IT VISIBLE

Now that you have your why, make it visible. Write it on a Post-it note and stick it on your computer, your desk, your bathroom mirror, your refrigerator, wherever you will see it each day. Be creative. Paint it on a canvas, create a poem or song about it, make a sticker and put it on your water bottle, write it on a piece of paper to fold and carry with you out in the world. Snap a photo of your why and make it your screen saver on your computer or your home screen on your phone. Make it visible so you can remember and receive energy from it.

IDENTIFY YOUR CURRENCY

Many of us would be pleased if we made some money from our writing. But money may or may not happen. However, there still needs to be an exchange for the writing to keep flowing. Otherwise, you may feel overwhelmed and overworked, frustrated, angry, and perhaps even ready to give it all up and try something else, like juggling fishbowls.

Let's find some other currencies you can receive from your endeavors. Besides money, what three things do you want to come from writing your story?

Here are some ideas:

- Advances your career
- Advances your sense of self
- Connects you with readers
- Contributes to your overall growth as a human being

- Creates passion in your life
- Gifts you the opportunity to learn new things and practice your craft
- Gives you a sense of purpose
- Grants you a better understanding of yourself and life
- Helps you see the world in a different way
- Helps you share what you have learned so others don't make the same mistakes
- Provides peace and clarity about your past

Once you identify your top three, imagine how you would feel if these happened. Come back to these time and again, visualizing them and keeping your focus on these coming true.

WRITE FROM YOUR HEART

You have the power to become aware of your inner landscape—your feelings, your inner themes, and your why. Take some time to be conscious of it by getting in touch with your heart. Imagine your heart is speaking to you, giving you the deep reasons for why you are writing. What do you feel? If you compare yourself to others, write to sell books, or to please someone else, you will be out of alignment. The truest place to write from is your heart. How do you do this? It's about trusting yourself. For some of us, it can take time to really trust ourselves as creators. Practice will help. Notice any part of you that feels unworthy or that you simply don't trust. Acknowledge it, and then see if you can shift your energy to something you have created, some skill or talent you have, or some beautiful vision that is dear to you. Embracing these will spark trust in your creative abilities and the heart-centered aspirations living inside you. Then, take the leap off the edge, and fall. Follow your sincerest why, your grandest passion. This is the true freedom of writing. In essence, writing from your heart will always be your best source of inspiration.

CHAPTER THREE

Be Intentional

Writing connects us. It connects us through space and time, to the ancient past and the distant future, to other ways of living, and to diverse thoughts, new ideas, and ourselves. Writing can connect us to parts of ourselves we didn't even know were there. Writing is a miracle, a time-traveling device, an oracle, a friend, and a gift for writers and for readers. People who cannot swim can be transported to the depths of the deep blue sea and float with ease. We can soar to other galaxies. We writers are honored to play in that vast space of creativity with all its endless possibilities.

To be connected with all this magic, we need one basic ingredient: intention. Each word asks us to be intentional. It's all about having a purpose, a meaning, or aim. It is the unseen significance beneath the words. Readers can't see it, but they can feel it.

Intention is different from your why. Your why fuels you and helps you see the reason you are a writer and why you are writing a particular piece. Being intentional is specific to each time you show up to write. It can stay the same or change over time.

Let me give you an example. Perhaps you are writing a chapter that is a pivotal moment in the book—a father is dying and realizes he can no longer protect his daughter. She will have to navigate the world without him. What is your intention for this? Why do you need to show this in the book? Is it the darkest moment? Is this pushing your main character to their limits so they can ultimately confront their deepest fears and doubts? While this is necessary to know for your story, it is even more important to know your intent for writing this in the first place. There is more to this scene than how it fits in the story. Why do you want to write this particular struggle? How does this theme show up in your story? How does it show up in your life? What do you know about this? And more importantly, why do you feel this is significant to write about?

You don't have to have a specific intention and answers to all these questions for every scene. But the more intentional you are for the biggest moments in your writing, the more realistic and resonant they will be for you and for your readers.

Intention leads us to theme. Theme is an underlying meaning or big idea you are exploring through your writing. Usually, we are drawn to write about certain themes. Theme drives everything. It's your message, what you want to convey and explore, what you'd like readers to connect with. If you are not sure about your theme, go back to your why. Why are you writing this piece? You could have chosen anything to write about, but you didn't choose those other subjects. You chose this one.

We all have our themes as writers. We gravitate to writing the same themes across all our writing, no matter how many different genres and forms we write in. Why? Because these themes are significant to us. By writing about them, we explore and learn. We get to know ourselves better and heal and solve and transform. Knowing our intent will reveal a lot about who we are and what we are seeking to discover through our writing.

One talented writer I have the pleasure to know shared her intention, theme, and why for writing her story about finding herself, getting past addiction, and coming to terms with her sexuality. This is what she told me:

> I write for myself, so I can understand my past and better understand myself. So I can heal and use the valuable lessons that led me to this point moving forward. So I can process and proceed in becoming the best version of myself. So I can view my flaws and imperfections compassionately. In the event my book is hopefully published one day … I write for others. For an audience that is receptive to self-compassion. For the world, so my stories may serve to connect us individuals as part of a greater whole. For anyone who has ever suffered through insecurity, divorce, sexuality issues, substance abuse, and leaving their career behind. To let them know they are not alone. To offer hope and inspiration for those that could use it.

She has strong, clear themes and intentions for her overall story and each time she writes. She knows her audience, her why, and what she intends to create. Her clarity of purpose, presence, and intentionality are inspiring.

One of my clients is writing a nonfiction book about how we handle change—a book I believe we all could benefit from. His theme is laser-focused, as are his whys and intentions. He has lots of real-world experience and a terrific new take on the type of mindset needed to shift from a place of fear to a proactive and empowering state. When I probed into what fuels him, this is what he told me:

> If a person wants to confront the demons of self-doubt and test their ability to persevere, they should commit to writing a book. Do I have anything to say? Is this even interesting? Does anyone care about this but me? The weight of commitment associated with writing a book is heavy. However, I intuitively know that the effort of writing it pales in comparison to the burden I will carry for the remainder of my life if I don't.

For fiction writers, our intentions can be a bit different. I have a beloved friend who reads and writes romance. She adores it (no pun intended) and loves happily ever afters. It feels good to her, gives her hope, and entertains her. She wants to create that for her readers because she believes we all deserve a happy ending. Each scene leads to something fulfilling. And the joy she derives from doing so is evident in how she talks about it. It lights her up.

Then there is an author I met who was writing historical fiction. Her prose was lovely and historically rich, and all the speech patterns, idioms, expressions, and descriptions of the time period were marvelous. What she was lacking was a deep connection with the main character. He wasn't likeable. This can be fine; we don't always have to like characters, but I didn't care about him at all. And many of her beta readers said the same thing. Yet no one could figure out why.

So, I asked her, "What was your intention for writing about this specific protagonist?"

She stayed quiet. "I'm not sure. I like the time period. I read his journals, and he fascinated me."

"But why? You could have chosen anyone in history. But you chose him. What did you want to convey to your readers? Why do you care? And why should your readers care?"

We delved deeper into the conversation, and she described his real-life character in an intriguing way—the relationships with his siblings, his passions, and most importantly, his motivations and goals for everything he was doing. Ah, now we were getting somewhere. That was all she needed. Off she went, deconstructing the aspects of his character that made her care about him, that would make readers care. In her rewrite, she injected those aspects throughout the story, crafting a much deeper and more intriguing character and keeping her intention clear the whole time.

I read draft two. What a difference. The protagonist had all the same attributes as before, but the veil had been lifted, and we saw his humanness. I cared and even rooted for him. A full transformation. This is what the upside of falling is all about. She was willing to take in what many early readers noticed wasn't working, look deeply within herself—her intentions and her why—let go, and then apply what she learned. Incredible.

Knowing what you want readers to experience will also help direct your writing. Consider what you want the reader to feel when reading your piece. How would you like them to feel at the end? What would you like them to gain from this experience? If readers were going to say something about your story to others, what would that be? Knowing these answers will help you infuse those elements into your piece.

Intentionality has many levels—the reason you are writing this piece, the reason it works within the story, the purpose it serves for the reader, and the purpose it serves for you.

Sometimes it's easy to identify your intention for writing. Other times it feels like looking for a specific grain of sand on a long stretch of beach. And it may change as you write your piece, from day to day. As long as it is genuine and feels good and fits that moment, go with it. Follow that positive energy. This is where the magic of connection begins to blossom.

What we feel when we write is a direct reflection of what is happening inside us. By tuning in and becoming aware of our bigger intention for writing, we take thoughtful and meaningful steps toward creating something with grander resonance. Be open and willing to receive whatever wants to come through you. Enjoy the discoveries. Those beautiful epiphanies come from present moment awareness and dedicated self-reflection.

Practice & Play

Here are some powerful ways to help you gain more clarity, connect with your intentions, and reveal more about your inner writer.

SET AN INTENTION

Setting an intention before you write helps you align your thoughts and actions with the present moment. When you are clear about your intention (for your whole book or even just a particular scene), you will start connecting with all the infinite possibilities for your writing, your readers, and yourself. Discovering your intention involves introspection. Take time to reflect on your motivations, aspirations, emotional state, and interest in certain topics and themes. Reflect on your audience—who are you writing for? Be specific. Whether you express these answers to your houseplants, keep them inside your mind, or write them out, affirm the connection you want with your writing. What if resistance comes up again? That's okay. Remember, it's common. It can take some time to trust what it is you feel and are wanting to explore. Sometimes we can even get lost in what our inner critic is saying since that voice can be quite loud. It's okay. It's part of the process. Take your time. When you feel ready, have a look at a few examples of intentions I've had over the years. Then, create yours.

- Craft my story with honesty and vulnerability so I can connect with readers on a more personal level.
- Develop a sense of place and time, vividly describing the setting, bringing it to life.

- Experiment with a new writing technique or narrative structure to challenge storytelling conventions.
- Have fun bringing my characters and my story to life.
- Hone my dialogue skills with authentic conversations that reveal character and move the story forward.
- Infuse my writing with emotion, exploring how this affects my characters and why it is important to me.
- Propel the story forward by introducing a key plot point or big conflict.
- Practice mindfulness and presence, immersing myself fully in the act of writing.
- Tap deeper into my imagination and enable my creativity to flow freely, uninhibited.
- Uncover truths about myself and the world around me by exploring a particular theme.
- Write unreservedly, without judgment, letting go of self-doubt and owning my story.

Now it's your turn.

- What is it I intend to explore, understand, and feel?
- What is it I intend to learn? To complete? To change?
- Why is this important to me?
- Why is this important to the readers?
- How do I feel when I express this intention?

VISUALIZE THE ESSENCE

Similar to setting an intention, positive visualization is a powerful tool to show you something is possible. It guides your subconscious to anticipate a positive outcome. It can also act as a road map to help you get there. Once you visualize something, it feels real, because it is. You made it so by bringing your awareness to it. There are many studies indicating that our brains believe what we visualize is real. You are in fact creating the reality before it happens. Visualization is rooted in neuroscience and psychology. When you vividly imagine an action, your brain activates similar neural pathways as when you actually perform it. For creative types like writers, visualization can be a powerful tool for enhancing creativity, boosting motivation and confidence, and helping you overcome any place you feel stuck. By regularly practicing visualization, you can improve your ability to bring ideas to life more vividly and effortlessly. Before you write, visualize what will be on the page. What does it look like? How long will it be? What do you want this particular writing experience to be like? Imagine how you'll feel at the end of it. Where do you want your story to end up? Just like when setting an intention, be specific and detailed to best create what it is you most desire.

ELEVATE YOUR ENERGY

Everything in this universe is made up of energy. Living beings, inanimate objects, and thoughts and emotions are composed of a universal energy. And so, it follows that words themselves have their own energy. We writers also bring our unique energy to our words. Check in with yourself and see what energy you bring to your writing. This is part of being intentional. Are you tired? Having trouble focusing? Hurried? Ambivalent? Frustrated? Angry? Or are you joyful? Excited? Devoted? Peaceful? Full of wonder? Notice where your energy is. By bringing your awareness to your mental, emotional, and even your physical state, you can begin to shift it to a higher, freer energy, one more in alignment with what you want to create. For example, if you're tired, maybe it's time to rest and practice some self-care before you write. If you are frustrated with the writing process and don't feel motivated, then perhaps it's time to step away from your piece. Consider what specifically is bothering you about your piece. Be curious. Curiosity operates at a higher frequency than frustration because it is a more expansive and open state of mind, whereas frustration is contractive and restrictive. Curiosity leads to exploration, possibility, and creativity. Frustration often leads to rumination and blockage, causing mental and emotional constriction. So, be curious, and notice what it is that you are bothered by and what you could change. And maybe you're feeling wonderful and ready—then, by all means, start writing. But no matter how incredible you feel, there is always another level up you can go.

DISCOVER YOUR THEME

As you look to discover what themes you are drawn to, you will better understand yourself and your writing. Start from the highest perspective you can, the big picture and what you instantly connect with. We can connect with many themes, but most likely one or two will have more energy for us. Here are the most common themes. Read through the list without much contemplation, and answer the inquiries by following your energy for what feels the most powerful and compelling.

Common Themes

- Belief vs. doubt
- Coming of age
- Courage and heroism
- Death

- Environmentalism
- Family and friendship
- Fate vs. free will
- Good vs. evil
- Identity
- Individual vs. society
- Justice
- Loneliness
- Love
- Perseverance
- Power and corruption
- Prejudice
- Redemption and revenge
- War vs. peace

Inquiries

- What are the top three themes I most relate to?
- Which one has the strongest energy behind it?
- Why is it important to me?
- Which one fits best for the piece I am writing?

These themes are general and important to know. However, see if you can be more specific. For example, you may resonate with the theme of love, but what kind of love? Romantic love, unrequited love, motherly love, love for the planet, loss of love, or self-love? Let's take self-love. Perhaps the part of self-love you want to explore is self-acceptance, learning to love yourself for who you are, ending the façade of people pleasing. The more specific and personal you can get with your theme, the more universal the message.

CHAPTER FOUR

Be Moved

There is nothing so horrible in my life that spending time with a sea otter can't improve. These adorable little beings light me up.

One time I was kayaking in central California, and a sea otter swam right up to me, only a few feet away. I stopped paddling and watched as the beautiful otter twirled, bathed, and floated. I could have watched all day, but another kayak came, and the otter swam away. I experienced so much joy by being present with the simplicity and grace of that amazing creature. From that encounter, I learned the essence of inspiration.

I was moved.

When we are moved, we are transported from one state of being to another. We are given access to a whole new world in the span of seconds. We are connected to more than the limited view we carry around. We gain a renewed sense of verve for life. We are excited and open to wonder.

As writers, we put a lot of pressure on ourselves to produce something, do it right, increase our word count, rewrite, finish our books, publish, market, sell, repeat. When we do this from a place of effort, the delight disappears. Effort replaces joy. We think we need to expend effort to accomplish something. That's not true. Less effort can bring forth more energy, creativity, and forward motion in our writing. Being inspired makes it so.

When we are truly inspired, our writing gushes out of us. Yes, we need a certain amount of time and energy to write, but it need not be an effort. It can be a flow derived from an inspired place where we feel moved.

The way to write from this place, to reduce effort and increase joy, is to seek those people, places, activities, and things that excite, ignite, and inspire you. They will give you energy, more ease, and more beauty with your words. Inspiration will lead you to that infinite source of energy within you. It will be what ultimately motivates your audience to read what you've created. That infectious energy will transmit through your words.

When we are struggling to write, it often means we are receiving one thing from our inspirations, but we are writing something else. Or we don't feel that our inspirations, and what we create from them, have any value. Or we are simply not inspired at all.

I met an incredibly talented literary fiction writer who didn't feel his words were worthy of sharing. He kept his book away from the world for more than a decade—he didn't even show it to his wife. Eventually, he entrusted me to edit his words and help him shape his story. I felt so grateful. His prose rivaled many literary legends. Although it did need some work, he reconnected with the beauty of why he was writing and was reinspired to finish the book. Through this journey, he was able to explore the possibilities of how it could live in the world.

Here is what he said when I asked him why he wrote:

> The story sings in me, and songs are meant to be sung—even if no one else is listening. I need the song. I am the song.

He radiated inspiration. He felt the song in him no matter what else would happen. That is pure inspiration and certainly one of the reasons his writing is so beautiful. He lives in his inspired space. He fosters it and nurtures it. He resides in the peace and joy between the words and the drafts and all the phases he and his project go through.

How else can we spark inspiration? We can read. This may seem obvious, and it is, but just because something is obvious doesn't mean it's not important. Have you ever read a book that changed your life? That moved you from one state of being to another? Books are like elixirs, gifting us what we need, often when we didn't even know we needed whatever it was that it was giving us.

I love books. I have so many favorites. Four stand out: *The Alchemist* by Paulo Coelho, *The Road* by Cormac McCarthy, *Johnny Got His Gun* by Dalton Trumbo, and *The Giving Tree* by Shel Silverstein. Why these? Each one moved me.

Coelho's *The Alchemist* offers storytelling as a vehicle for personal transformation. The novel's blend of fable-like simplicity and deep philosophical themes demonstrates how universal truths can be woven into a compelling narrative. Each time I read it I feel inspired to delve deeper into my own journey of self-discovery. It is also a reminder that all humans share similar struggles, hopes, and dreams.

In *The Road*, Cormac McCarthy's stark, poetic prose demonstrates the raw emotional depth of a father and son's journey through a desolate world. The novel's minimalistic yet powerful language creates tension and evokes deep empathy with few words. This book inspires me to strip down my writing to its most essential elements—proving that silence and simplicity can carry as much weight as action. Much like in life.

Then there's Dalton Trumbo's controversial book *Johnny Got His Gun*. I read it in high school. Wow. This novel's unflinching portrayal of war's horrors, told through the mind of a soldier trapped in his own body, challenges readers. Trumbo's relentless first-person perspective, where the protagonist's thoughts become the reader's prison, is a deep psychological immersion into some of life's most harrowing truths. I couldn't help but feel intense empathy, anger, sorrow, and a myriad of other emotions. I was definitely moved and have never forgotten the way I felt reading the ending pages of that book. They are unapologetic, visceral, and so beautifully written. I can't imagine my life without having had that experience.

Unlike *The Alchemist*—a cherished book I've read several times—I could not see reading *The Road* or *Johnny Got His Gun* again. The emotional darkness is too haunting for me to revisit. But I am forever grateful for the experience I had with those words. They have changed me for the better.

Lastly, but not leastly (I know that's not a word, but I feel like it should be), there is my childhood favorite book, *The Giving Tree*, by Shel Silverstein. His sparse, childlike prose carries deep themes about unconditional love and self-sacrifice. I cry each time I read it. That tree is so sweet. Goodness. This book also reminds me that storytelling doesn't need complexity to resonate—sometimes, the most profound truths are those that are humble and that speak directly to our hearts.

The books I have shared hold a special place in my life. Each one has gifted me something intangible and priceless. They have moved me. This is what we get to do as writers. What an honor to create such works of art.

What books have moved you? What else in your life creates that kind of shift for you? How can you spark inspiration for yourself so you can create your most inspired prose? These are the inquiries we need to be asking ourselves. How can we inspire ourselves so we can inspire others?

Let's talk for a moment of containers. A container is a book, chapter, scene, page, or word count that holds your story. Don't write to fill a container. If you limit yourself to that, then you will feel constrained. Write first from the concept and inspiration, then when you revise and edit, you can fulfill the needs of the container. In other words, let the container overflow to start.

Of course, it's good to have some knowledge of the container, but then let that go. How do you do this? Abide by your characters, story, and feelings while you're writing rather than being directed by how many pages you believe you need to write. Follow the positive energy and what feels right for the piece. You will notice the difference because it will feel more organic instead of forced.

The main point is to follow your inspiration. Don't just sit and write; sing your song on the page. Bring your words to life because you can't imagine tucking them away and keeping them inside. Go into the world and find what lights you up, and bring that energy back to the page. It may not be sea otters, but whatever it is, go find it. Venture out into the world, both real and imaginary, and build your energy. Fill yourself up and nourish your creativity by finding what feeds you. Not only will you feel the wave of fulfillment in your writing and your life, but you will also no longer feel the effort. You will feel the ease, the joy.

You will be moved.

Practice & Play

Being inspired is one of the most beautiful experiences we can have. It's that tingle, that uplifting feeling, that "aha" moment of knowing we are connected to more than our tiny self on this beautiful planet spinning through the universe. There are boundless ways to be inspired. Here are a few to help you ignite that spark of inspiration within you. Delve into these but also create your own. Ask a friend; see what they do for inspiration. Go and seek inspiration. It is waiting for you.

TAKE YOUR WORDS FOR A WALK

Instead of sitting down to write, take your words for a walk. Take them around with you as you go out and travel. Either mentally or written down, carry them with you. You are purposefully taking your writing with you so you can discover the depths of what you long to convey. Nature enhances creativity. Movement does, too. Look around—see your story in the sky, your characters in the trees, or your theme in the car rushing by. Follow your instincts and see what comes up for you around the piece you are writing. Be willing to let go of any attachments to what will happen. Simply be on your walk, open and ready to receive.

BLEND YOUR INSPIRATIONS

Inspiration is not linear or singular. Learn to blend your inspirations and let them overlap and move you in ways you wouldn't ordinarily think they would. For instance, I love to listen to world music and sing when I write. I often don't know the language of the artist or know how to pronounce the words, but the melody, rhythms, and strong emotions get me moving. I sing along and dance in my seat and move my fingers along the keys with ease. I jump up and down when I complete a scene. I doodle when I need some motivation. While contemplating my next line, I skip around my living room. I practice yoga between writing scenes or bake some new treat while brainstorming my next chapter. I watch a scene from a movie or flip randomly through a book and read a page for inspiration. I talk to my cat—yes, yes, I do.

Writing, and just writing, can feel stale sometimes. Expand your ideas of what could inspire you. It doesn't have to be some grandiose experience like a trip to Antarctica or a Broadway show. It can be small, a day-to-day occurrence. A conversation with a friend about what lights them up. A sprouting blossom in your garden. A new recipe. Humming, chanting, playing an instrument, sculpting, drawing, assembling jigsaw puzzles, breaking the Guinness World Record for unicycling (it's about eighteen miles traveled in one hour), or whatever.

Know that other art forms can play a symbiotic role in creation. Blend your inspirations together. Go back and forth between two or three. Be with more than one art form at a time; take from one art and give to another. Stretch beyond the ordinary. Find what inspires you.

To help you along, here are some questions to explore:

- What other art form can inspire my writing?
- What new activities can I add to my writing practice to give me a boost?
- What if I wrote in a different genre or style?
- What type of visual art, like painting, sculpture, or photography, can I use for inspiration?

- What tastes or smells can inspire a fresh idea?
- What kind of new music or sounds can I listen to while I am writing that may stimulate my creativity?
- What new places or settings captivate me, and how can I incorporate those into my writing process?
- What other authors or books have left a lasting impression on me that I can use for inspiration?
- How can I use nature and the outdoors as a source for inspiration?

STOP WRITING

You know why you have that great idea when you are soaking wet in the shower and have just lathered your hair with shampoo? It's because you are free from trying to make the words come. You have given them room. Creativity needs space and time. Give yourself that. It is an ebb and flow. You'll go through magical, productive times when you can't stop writing and other times when nothing comes out. If the well is dry, fill yourself back up. We can't exhaustively create. We need to recharge and bring new life to our process.

Sometimes the best thing we can do is not write. Step away and let your story marinate until you can't wait to get back to it. Do something else, anything, that brings you joy. Your story will be working in the background, gaining momentum. Then, one day, the energy will be so strong it will be all you can think about. You will have inspiration to write. That is the organic way inspiration works. It can't be forced; it needs to be nurtured. And if for some reason you are still not feeling inspired, don't fret. Keep opening yourself to new activities, words, and ideas. Be out in the world and let yourself be moved by its wonders. The laughter of a child, the rustle of leaves in the wind, the golden hues of a sunset—let these moments seep into you. Inspiration is not something we chase; it's something we invite. Trust that your words will return when they are ready, grander, and more alive because you have given them time to breathe. So, step away when you need to, knowing that, in stillness, your creativity is quietly gathering its strength. And when the time comes, you will write again—more powerfully than before.

WRITE FOR FREE

If you get paid to write, fantastic. For others, writing is a passion that doesn't bring in a steady paycheck. Sometimes, it's done for free. But if you think about it, writing is not truly free. There is a cost of time and energy. Sometimes we get bogged down with the idea that writing takes too much time and energy, and we aren't getting anything from it, at least not financially.

What if we shift our mindset to be in the joy of writing and do it for nothing, just because we love it so much? When did you stop writing for joy? When did it become a commodity? Something to sell? Something you needed someone else to like? Something you needed something from?

Can you see that when you don't ask anything from it, writing frees you? It is a gift of inspiration. We get to spend our time aligned to this uplifted space. Free yourself by writing for free. Consider these inquiries:

- What do I feel writing can free me from?
- How do I feel freer in my life because of my choice to write?

PART TWO

Innovation

The way things are is not where they need to stay. It is not where they are meant to stay. You get to make it so.

CHAPTER FIVE

Be Curious

In writing circles, there is much talk about writing what we know. That is important. Writing from experience and knowledge gives a truthful quality and depth to our writing. But think about how much we learn and grow when we write. Write what you know, yes, but also, write what you *want* to know. Do you want to know more about sea otters (I know you do)? Write about them. Write about black holes, the fjords in Iceland, or why asparagus makes our pee smell. When we are curious or fascinated with something, we are drawn to learn more. The more we explore, the more doors and windows open. Instead of needing something to be a certain way, we give ourselves license to play. There is always room for playfulness in writing. Play leads to joy.

One of the best things about curiosity is there are no rules or guidelines. We don't have to understand why we are curious or interested in something. We need only to follow that interest. Some writers ask me how they can be more adventurous in their writing, and here's my response: Be curious. Be fascinated. Lose yourself in the realms of discovery. You are an explorer, and your compass is the way you feel on the journey. If you start feeling tight or restricted, discouraged, or bored, take a step back. If you find joy and flow and energy, keep going. The adventure is the treasure of writing. See where it takes you.

Where to start? Anywhere. You don't have to start on page one. Start where you are. Start where you feel the most passion. It doesn't matter where you begin. You're going to end up somewhere different anyway. Trust your instincts and whatever emerges in the process. Don't overthink it. Be open and make room for something new.

Being curious is about opening ourselves up to possibilities. We notice new things, and our minds become more active, engaging in all sorts of ideas and different ways of being. If we approach our writing and life from a place of apathy or disinterest, we close ourselves off to infinite potential. When we shift to being inquisitive, we question everything and find wonderment in all that can be.

When we are curious, we are in awe of discovery. We try something new or something old in a different way. Following our curiosity can be exciting and rewarding because it expands our knowledge, skills, and perspective. With curiosity, it's not about getting something right. There is nothing to get right, and there is nothing to get wrong. It's about seeing what happens. From this expansive place, we develop as writers and have more to offer our readers.

The key is this: Be willing to fall. I don't use the word "fail" because there is no failure in writing, no matter what that persnickety eleventh-grade English teacher said. You are falling through a world of creativeness. Let go of what you've been gripping tightly. Allow your curious heart to take you to all kinds of wild and intriguing spaces in the outer world and within yourself. When you pursue what fascinates you, your passion for writing (and for this wondrous sojourn on earth) will soar.

Here's one of my favorite examples of curiosity in motion. I was working as a coach at a local writing retreat, and I met a newbie writer. She was shy and tentative about her writing, but she exuded excitement and passion for her story and her writing process. I had a one-on-one evaluation with her to discuss her idea for her children's book. This is what she shared with me:

> When my husband and I met, he had never been married and did not have any kids. Although I thought I was done having babies, falling in love changed all that. He wanted a family, and I wanted him. So, together, we made a wish, a wish to have a child together. Then one day, I was taking a walk through my neighborhood, marveling at the wish that was growing inside of me, when I had a thought … a realization.
>
> It occurred to me that we are all born into a world of wishes. Long before we enter this world, others are making wishes for us. It starts with our mom. Ideally, when a woman finds out she is pregnant, it is a wish come true … Now my daughter was about to be born into this world of wishes. A world that I and others were creating based on the many hopes, dreams, and wishes we had for her.

> It was then that I first thought about writing a story about a young girl named Maija who stumbles across her mom's journal. In this journal, Maija's mom has written down many of the wishes she has for her daughter. As Maija is reading through the journal in her backyard, a large gust of wind snatches it from her grasp and begins to tear out the pages one by one. The pages twist, turn, and expand to form steps, pieces of a gigantic staircase that spirals and ascends toward the sky. This staircase leads Maija to a magical world: A World of Wishes.

This writer followed her curiosity and developed a beautiful story, complete with a vivid world and fantastic characters. All this from one idea while she was on a walk. She pursued her fascination, and it led her to what will be a heartwarming and memorable book.

Part of being curious is about being willing to challenge ourselves, our creativity, and our reluctance to live outside the lines. That is the beauty of writing—you never know what will happen or where it will take you. Remember, there are no correct answers when it comes to writing. Instead, there is only what is fulfilling for you. Even then, a multitude of possibilities surface.

How do we build curiosity? Simple. We ask questions. I like to use "What would happen if" questions. What would happen if I deleted this scene? What would happen if I added a paragraph here? If I changed these words around? If I added a new character? If I switched these chapters?

If I changed the tone of the book? If I explored a new topic here? If I researched this topic and added details?

I also like to use "I wonder." I wonder if this scene is necessary. I wonder what it would add to my story if I changed this to that. I wonder how it would feel if I tried this. I wonder if it would flow better if I switched these words. I wonder if I started here instead of there—how would that be? Use "What would happen if" and "I wonder" questions to guide you to new places.

Another enjoyable way to spark curiosity in our writing is to reconnect with our love of words. There are more than 170,000 words in the English language, in current use. Why not discover some new ones? Seek out new words like you would a pair of shoes. See if they fit. How do they sound? Do they inspire you? What do they spark in you? How can you invite them into your writing? What can you learn from them? If you're writing fiction, are you daring enough to make up new words and phrases? What about new fictitious character names and places? Be zany, imaginative, or intellectual. Be adventurous.

The main takeaway is this: Both the fictitious character Curious George and all the cats that ever lived are led by fascination. They have a sense of wonder, and they follow it.

We can't arrive somewhere new if we aren't willing to see what is out there. How can we push the boundaries of who we are and what we know and what we write if we don't maintain a high level of curiosity? We can't craft compelling prose from a place of disinterest or routine. We need to break free of the constraints of what we believe exists and shift to believing in what *could* be there.

Be curious. Be fascinated. That will get you to where you want to be. And you'll have a lot more fun along the way.

Practice & Play

Curiosity is a lot like creativity. If you don't practice it, it fades. Here are a few ways to foster your fascination and get yourself moving in fun and inspired directions.

DO THE OPPOSITE

Often, we are drawn to certain tendencies. We choose to use the same words over and over again, the same tone, the same types of stories, the same sentence structure and length, the same way of constructing dialogue. It's important to identify some of your tendencies and stretch yourself to new places. One way to do this is by doing the opposite. Ask "What is the opposite of what I would normally want to do or think to do?" Try it; see how it feels. This creates movement in your writing. It shows you the other side, an alternate reality. Pay attention to the way it feels and what happens when you make this change. For example, instead of a narrative unfolding in chronological order, it can start at the end and work backward. A coming-of-age story not about a teenager but an elderly person who realizes it's not too late to change their life. Or if you are prone to writing shorter, choppy sentences with a fast pace, try a slower, more descriptive style. Change up your theme, or reverse your character's motivations. Opposites can add depth, surprise, and novelty to your writing. Sometimes doing the opposite will help you realize what you have is working. And sometimes just the opposite.

LEARN FROM YOUR CHARACTERS

We can learn a lot from what and who we are writing about. Make a list of all your main characters. Reflect on your characters as you answer the following questions. Write to each of these, and see what you learn. And yes, this practice works for most genres, including memoir. You and all the people in your story can be your biggest teachers.

- What do my characters need from me to come to life?
- What do the readers want from them?
- What do the characters have to teach me?
- What do I need from them?
- What do they add to the story?
- Why are they important for me to write about?

AFFIRM CURIOSITY

If you are feeling uninterested, without a kernel of curiosity, and you need a little oomph to get you going, try affirming any or all of these statements that resonate with you. For some, fill in the blanks. Say them out loud with positive energy. See where you are led and what changes inside you.

- I am curious.
- I am fascinated to see how this all unfolds.
- I am bold and willing to try new things.
- I am excited to know more about ______________________ ____.
- I want to try a new writing technique, particularly ____.
- I have always been fascinated by the topic of ______________________ and want to learn more.
- I am intrigued by the idea of ______________________ ____.
- I am ready to be more adventurous in my writing, and I am starting by______________________________.

INTERVIEW YOURSELF

One of my favorite discoveries is the benefit of interviewing myself. I had hit a rough patch in a piece I was writing. One of my strengths is answering questions. So, I interviewed myself about what I was writing. What happened was amazing. This piece I had struggled with for weeks flowed out of me in two hours. Ask yourself some interview questions to get to the heart of what you are writing and how to move forward with your project. What's the point? Why are you writing about this? What is happening in this piece? What do you most want to convey? What do you want readers to learn? What experience do you want to have with this piece? What is the reason you have that character in your book? Why that setting? What is the importance of that theme to you? What could you add to enhance your theme? What are you most fascinated about in this story? Answer these questions and add any of your own to build your curiosity.

CHAPTER SIX

Be Guided by Surprise

Now that you're curious and fascinated, let's talk about one of life's biggest challenges: the unknown. This aspect of being human can cause us a lot of grief. We like knowing things—everything, really. We aren't okay with mystery unless we are reading one. But here's the key: We can't and don't have to know everything, or anything at all, to move forward. Many times, having an answer is not possible. But we often hinge our willingness to move onward, our ability to be at ease, or our happiness on obtaining answers.

What if, instead, you could be guided by surprise?

Life is mysterious. That isn't going to change. Some things we will discover, and others will always be unknown. When we embrace not having the answers, we enjoy the fall. We don't know where we're falling to, but that's okay. It's exciting, and this element of surprise is what brings us into the present moment.

It can feel scary to plunge into something without knowing. The mind wants to know and tries to hold on as you're falling. Life is a process of discovery. So is being a writer. To write, you don't need to know everything.

Watching as something is revealed is part of the joy of reading and the joy of creating. Give yourself space and time to not know. Be in love with the mystery. Let go of expectations to have answers, and embrace not knowing. Be willing to adjust as surprise takes you by the hand and leads you down unexpected roads. There are so many doors to open. Delight in not knowing what is behind them. Just start opening doors. Let your readers revel in the mystery, too.

How can we do this? Start by committing to something we can't quite grasp yet. This doesn't mean we'll never outline or brainstorm. When in the flow of creation, we are first and foremost an innovator, and great innovators take leaps and fall into the unknown. They don't know where they are going to end up. Often it is somewhere better than they could have planned. Have you ever started with a plan, then written something, and it turned into something else entirely? I have. It often feels wonderful to venture deeper into the writing, bringing me deeper into falling. It's my favorite part of the writing process. Before I sit down to write, I wonder: What is going to happen today?

Many of us fear what we cannot see, hear, or understand. We are constantly seeking answers to something. Not everything in life is concrete or comes with empirical evidence. It's time to not only accept but also see the value in the unknown. Ask: Why do I feel the need to know something? What could I gain if I let go and trust surprise as my guide? Another way to look at it is this: If you do not have an absolute yes or no in your heart, do not decide. Be in the unknown. Wait and be open to answers.

Be flexible and bendable. Be willing to stretch and move and go down new pathways toward your ending. A rigid course will stifle you. It's an awful burden to strive to make something happen the way you imagined. That's rarely a recipe for innovation or joy.

When we are in the flow of life, with our words moving through us, that is where the magic happens. I've used the phrase "in the flow" before. What do I mean by this?

Imagine you decide to go swimming in Fiji. There is a warm tropical breeze, and the sun shines down as you're standing on the edge of a cliff. You look around. You want to be in the ocean, but you don't want to fall. The only way to get into the water is to jump. After a few moments, you hold your breath and go for it. While you're in the air, you try everything you can to not fall. Of course, this doesn't work. All you're doing is resisting what is happening. Being in the flow is the opposite of resistance. It is knowing that the fall *is* the flow. Being in the ocean is wonderful, but being in the air—that is pure exhilaration. If you just walked right up to the water and waded in, chances are you wouldn't appreciate the water as much or be as present as you would if you had fallen from a great height into it. The more you flex and bend to the moment, the more your creation will come alive. The more you will come alive, too, often in ways you never expected.

One of my favorite writers I've worked with was writing a memoir about spending time in prison for a crime he didn't commit. He was a fantastic writer and a witty and intelligent guy. His story, however, was unfocused. We brainstormed what he wanted to convey in his book, trying to pinpoint the main theme. After some coaching, he jumped in and explored many different directions his story could go. In one of our sessions, I asked a lot of questions. He willingly followed. Then, in one beautiful moment, it became clear to me how his unconnected stories fit together. His book wasn't about the time he spent in prison; it was about all the prisons he put himself in over the years—before, during, and after his incarceration. The theme was about not accepting or loving himself. That's what landed him in prison and what continued to keep him locked up until he realized it and set himself free. We discovered the heart of his story and the heart of why he was writing his story but also what he had endured and how he could heal. The fall into those memories and life challenges from his past ultimately brought him inner peace and freedom. And an incredible ending to the book.

We all have our own flow and arrive at it differently. The one requirement is to let go of control and not worry about the outcome. The outcome is in the future, and by focusing on it, you won't be fully present. While reading a book, do you think only about the ending? Of course not. That's not enjoyable. You read for the journey, the experience, the way it feels, the surprises along the way. It's no different being the writer. Write for the unknown. Most importantly, be comfortable with these three words—I don't know. Saying "I don't know" opens us up. By affirming these words, we're empowered to go on an adventure. We encounter new experiences and insights. We may discover that we'll never know the answer. That in itself is an exploration. Besides, how boring would writing and life be if we knew everything? Not only is that impossible, but it's also certainly not any fun.

Writing has a distinct life of its own. When we set aside preconceived ideas and are guided by surprise, there is space for something new. Something unexpected. We are inspired. We are pioneers. We are innovators.

Practice & Play

Surprise! Here are some practices to get you into the flow of your writing and open you to unexpected turns and joys. Okay, maybe it's not much of a surprise since I have these at the end of every chapter, but that proves my point. The expected is not that exciting. However, you don't know what these practices will be, so, like jumping off a cliff, they include the element of anticipation.

SHAKE IT UP

We love our routines. Our favorite mug of tea sitting on our desk at just the right angle. We wear our lucky blue T-shirt that says "I am strong," and we have our favorite snacks, music, and rituals before we engage with our words. These are all fine. But what if I told you routines often mean we are not conscious? When we have a routine, we are set in a certain way of viewing and being. This limits our perspective and ability to go with the surprises waiting for us. You can't get somewhere new if you try to move in the same patterns and actions of your past. To ignite your creativity, mix things up. Explore different ways to shake up your writing sessions. Use these inquiries and see how you can change your routine. Sometimes it takes just one or two things. Don't let those become routine, either. Find ways to continually tweak your writing sessions so you are fresh and full of new energy.

- How can I shake up my writing routine?
  Examples: Change your writing space, alter your writing schedule, use different tools for a session, write using a timer for shorter bursts to motivate you.

- What is something I can let go of?
  Examples: Perfectionism—your first draft need not be flawless; writing is a process. Rigid outlines—relax those tight restraints you've placed on your story. Distractions—put away your phone and stay away from the internet. Repetitive phrases or clichés—you know, the ones that don't add much. Guilt for taking breaks—resting is necessary for creativity, so let go of the guilt when you need some time to rest.
- What is something different I can try?
  Examples: Writing in a different genre. Collaborative writing. Different points of view. Prompts and creative exercises. Good old-fashioned handwritten text.
- What have I always wanted to try but never had the courage to until now?
  Examples: Attending a writing retreat or conference. Writing a personal story/memoir piece. Writing a fiction piece. Sharing my work in public at a reading or open mic night. Joining a writers' group. Creating a writing group. Submitting a piece for publication.

SAY YES, AND ...

In improv, there is a rule called, "Yes, and ..." It means accepting whatever was stated and expanding on that. You can't say "no" or "but," you must say "yes." For instance, if one person says, "I'm trapped in a peanut and the flying squirrels are coming to get me," the other person must accept this world and add to it. "Hold still, I've got this handy gigantic nutcracker." This goes back and forth and all the while, each performer follows the lead of what was shared. This can be a valuable practice to help you let go and be guided by surprise. Practice saying "Yes, and ..."

with your writing. See where it leads. You can even get other writers or friends involved and play with this prompt.

CHANGE YOUR LANGUAGE

We have a lot of programmed language that keeps us feeling small and in the perceived safety of our writing routines. Our self-talk can deflate, harm, and keep us stuck, causing fears that we aren't good enough or don't know how to write. The mind is full of stories and ways to keep us from being adventurous and embracing the mysterious. What if you had the power to change this? Excellent news—you do. You can replace these old stories and create new, more affirming thoughts. It's one of the most empowering things you can do for yourself. The first step is to notice some of the self-talk that is detrimental. Once you recognize it, you can notice that the mind is doing it and that it's untrue. Then, you can replace it with empowering words. It can feel challenging to go from your programmed negative self-talk straight to something positive. Again, notice any resistance. What do you feel? See if you can tap into what is behind your resistance. Be honest and open with this exploration. And if going from negative all the way to positive feels like too much of a fall, start with a more neutral approach, acknowledging this part of you that needs a bit more attention. Here are some examples of the old, negative ways of thinking. Each one is followed by a corresponding new way of viewing the same thought:

Old–New

- I can't—I am open to trying
- I am not as good as those other writers—I am learning, and embrace the process

- I don't know how—I enjoy not knowing because it's fun to discover something new
- I need to be perfect—I am perfectly imperfect
- I need to try harder—I am happy with whatever I am able to accomplish
- I have to get this to work—I am open to new and unexpected possibilities
- I am never going to finish this—I am excited about the journey
- I am not good enough—I am enough just as I am
- I don't have what it takes—I have everything I need inside me
- What I have to say doesn't matter—There is value in what I have to say
- I am going to fail—I am enjoying the fall and excited by all the surprises

LET GO OF PLANS

Plans are helpful when you're an architect or an event planner. Even these professionals know that sometimes what they painstakingly plan doesn't come to fruition. If you're the planning type, if you like to outline how everything is going to go, great. If that's part of your process, enjoy it. Once you're finished making those plans, let them go. Even those of us with more simplistic and relaxed outlines can let go of our preconceived ideas. We don't have any control over the future of our words. We don't know how they will all work or not work, who will be drawn to read them, or what will even happen at the end of our story. Whether you are a strict outliner or more of a free-falling kind of writer, practice making plans and letting them go. See what happens. Will everything go as planned? If it does, fantastic. If it doesn't, fantastic. Something even better is waiting for you. This requires a certain level of openness and detachment. Are you willing to follow the mystery? Practice this as you create, planning and letting go. It gets easier and more freeing as you build what I call your "letting go" muscles.

CHAPTER SEVEN

Be a Turtle

Turtles are fascinating. There are more than 350 different species of turtles. Leatherback turtles are the oldest reptiles, having been around since the dinosaurs. Turtle shells have sixty bones, and turtles don't have ears but are not deaf. Sea turtles can stay underwater for up to five hours by slowing their heart rate to about one beat every nine minutes. They love to travel—diving depths of up to 950 feet and swimming about 10,000 miles a year. Turtles have even traveled into space—probably not their plan, but hey.

You can see the rabbit (or turtle) hole I went down researching for this chapter. That's part of the falling—the unfolding adventure stemming from the kernel of an idea.

In this case, I came up with an idea: Turtles can travel only when they stick their necks out.

Being a writer is the same. We can't go far or deep in our writing without sticking our necks out. We need to be vulnerable. We need to open ourselves up. As writers, we want people to feel something, to connect to something beyond our words. The only way we can evoke emotions and connections with our readers is to put ourselves out there.

Staying in your shell won't get you far. Don't hide behind your words; push through them. Go as far as you can go, then go farther. Leave yourself on the page, the dark, raw, unseen parts of you. That is what people will remember.

Ask yourself, Can you go farther? Deeper? Is there more to be excavated? How far can you stretch your neck out? What's holding you back?

I am often asked at events or book signings how I handled writing the darkest moments of my life. It wasn't easy. First, I used a pseudonym to write the most difficult scenes. I called myself Maya. Having her as a character helped distance me from the horrific things I endured. Still, as my first book was about to come out, with all these raw, vulnerable pieces of me strewn about, I got nervous. I asked my writing group what I should do about my name.

"You guys think I should publish under the name Maya, or use my real name?"

The room was quiet. These talented writing buddies of mine were never shy with their words. But I could hear the cat breathing in the other room.

I surveyed my friends. They were different types of people writing a wide variety of books: historical fiction, romance, screenplays, satire, horror, and genre fiction. I was writing memoir, narrative nonfiction, and nonfiction. The beauty of our group was that we all had different viewpoints and whys for writing. The variety of our creations and feedback complemented one another. Because of them, I grew in my understanding of the craft and who I was with my words. They consistently helped me reach my highest potential.

After what felt like minutes, the horror writer in the room finally spoke. "Cherie, after everything that has happened to you, you're afraid to put your name on your book?"

There it was. My invitation to stick my neck out. My story would be more powerful and reach more people because I was willing to do that. Excellent advice.

If you're struggling with being vulnerable, ask yourself what can be gained from putting your neck out and what will be lost by staying inside your shell.

It's not just in memoir and nonfiction that we need to be like a turtle and stick our neck out. Fiction authors benefit from this just as much. A dear friend of mine—and one of my favorite writing peeps—was working on her debut novel the same time I was writing my memoir. Looking back, we both agree that we wouldn't have finished our books and executed them as well as we did without each other's help. She watched and supported me as I put myself out there, the honest and raw parts of my life that were hard to think about, let alone craft into a story. And I saw her stretch herself writing an outlandish but artfully written paranormal romance. Her book explored ancient aliens, conspiracy theories, UFOs, Sumerian cuneiform texts, the meaning of life, and a crazy human-alien romance. Is this the most popular topic? Nope. Relatable to everyone? Hardly. I hadn't heard of much of this until I met her. But she was all in. No holding back. She put herself, her beliefs, and her ideas out there. We even promoted our books together at festivals with an Aliens and Inspiration booth. Our books, intentions, whys, and audiences couldn't have been more different, but I am a better writer for knowing her. What a gift it was to see someone so dedicated to their craft.

Now, you may be surprised that I didn't mention that turtles are slow, since that's generally what most people think of when they talk about turtles. Sure, they are slow, but it's their pace that's important. Steady.

One of the challenges of being a writer is that writing is a big investment of our time. Writing is generally a slow process. Even if you were Stephen King, you could write only a couple of books a year.

Quality writing takes time, often a long time. We can feel impatient, like we are waiting for something to bloom. Because we are. If we rush or try to move through it, we evolve past it. When we slow down and sink into the flow of our process, we glean much more. Our steady pace feels not so slow. You know that feeling when you are in the moment and time ceases to matter? You are blissfully lost in the flow. You lose track of time. You don't notice anything other than the precious moment in front of you. That is the beauty of a steady pace. You are enjoying your surroundings and the world you are in. You don't want to rush. You like where you are.

I am a recovering fast mover. I used to move so fast I would often hold my breath and rush to and from each and every activity. I was the hare, or the Energizer Bunny. I kept going and going. But what I was really doing was burning out. Instead of being more productive, I was generating stress, anxiety, and lapses in focus. When I got really sick and was bedridden, I was forced to learn the art of slowing down and doing nothing. Over time, I saw the benefits of moving slower. We think speed and moving fast are always better. They're not. When you slow down, you become more present, which increases clarity. It enables you to appreciate the view and the sharp details in front of you, and it will help you make more intentional choices.

When I started embracing my inner turtle, my creativity skyrocketed. I stopped rushing, and my mind had space to wander, making unexpected connections and generating new ideas. Slowing down helped regulate my nervous system, lowering stress and bringing me a sense of calm. I became more productive. My focus was better, and I worked more efficiently. Rushing had led me to exhaustion, whereas a steady pace led me to improving the quality of my writing. I also gained a deeper sense of fulfillment because I was no longer chasing my goals but appreciating the slower, more peaceful time as I wrote.

Even now I am reminding myself to slow down. It is a daily practice. I often ask myself, How can I slow down and make more easeful choices for my writing and my life? Slowing down and being steady may seem counterintuitive, but try it. You may be amazed just how good it can feel.

Remember, turtles may seem slow, but inch by inch, they are getting where they want to go, sticking their necks out and gifting the world their stoic and strong presence.

Practice & Play

Vulnerability is often seen as a weakness. Actually, it can be a strength. When we are vulnerable in our writing, and in life, what we are really saying is "Here I am—scars, fears, flaws, and all, and I know you have them, too." Let's open up to what we all know is happening beneath our protective shells. This connects us to the world and to our writing and creates the most powerful prose. Here are some practices to connect you back to yourself and your process.

GO ALL IN

Going "all in" is a phrase in poker that means placing all your chips into the pot. When you go all in, you risk everything. You either win the hand or are out of the game. I used to play a lot of poker, and I see this similarity with writing. When you feel the energy and joy of writing, nothing is gained by holding back. Go all in with your writing, and see where it can take you. If you risk nothing, you risk a lot more. How do you go all in? Wherever you are, when you think you've gone as far as you can go, go one step farther, then another. Keep seeing how much more you can excavate those raw and naked parts of you. The stuff we hold fear or shame around—those aspects are the beauty that brings the world together. Those parts are waiting to be released.

KNOW THYSELF

One way to become more comfortable with being vulnerable is by getting to know yourself. You can do this by identifying and becoming more familiar with your strengths and weaknesses. Strengths are great; when you know what they are, you feel more positive and assured, and you can utilize them well. When you feel not good enough, or when you need an injection of confidence, take stock of your strengths. What might these be? Good vocabulary, discipline, creativity, and great dialogue? Fantastic. Play into those. Now, our weaknesses are important to look at, too. I don't like the word "weaknesses," but I think about it this way: These are simply muscles you haven't thought about or developed yet. With time and attention, they can be turned into strengths. These weaker spots are a gateway to growth and becoming more connected with your authentic self.

Make two separate lists, one with all your writing strengths and one with all your weaknesses. Take time and be with these lists. Seeing these written out can help you see all the opportunities ahead and the growth you've already had on your writing journey. How do you feel reading the strengths? How about the weaknesses? Pick one of these that you would like to explore, so it can become a strength. Take note that not all weaknesses can be changed. And that's absolutely okay. Focus on those you can change and accept the rest, knowing you will need help with those along the way. That's what editors, beta readers, and writing coaches are for. And dear friends.

IDENTIFY YOUR VULNERABLE AREAS

Being willing to pour your heart onto the page is not always easy, but it's worthwhile. No one wants to read about a perfect world or perfect character. We read to see the imperfections and grow from those. We yearn to see the vulnerability of the world and the people in it. This helps us with our own vulnerabilities. If you're writing memoir or nonfiction, you have a golden chance to share some of your deepest wounds and all the light you derived from them. Without sharing the wounds, the insights and wisdom don't mean as much. In fiction, the same applies. You can put your life lessons into the story and characters by opening up and delivering what is burning inside you. Your vulnerability is a gift to your prose and to all those who encounter it. Most importantly, it will feel like a gift to yourself. Take some time to sit with these inquiries to see how you can open up to the idea of being more vulnerable when you write.

- What do I need to feel safe (comfortable, at ease, relaxed) when I write?
- How can I be more vulnerable when I write?
- What do I need to let go of to write from this more vulnerable place?
- What is one step I can take to move onward, slow and steady, with courage and openness? How can I support myself through this step?

STEADY YOURSELF

I used to believe the faster I moved, the more I could get done. But I came to notice the faster I moved, the more I missed, fumbled, and jumbled things. Moving too quickly often made something take longer. And I was holding my breath, a lot. Ask yourself: Am I rushing? Holding my breath? Am I trying to get to the end of something?

When we stop the cycle of rushing, we can be more present and vulnerable. We notice more and are more open. Our writing glides because we let go of that frenetic energy and replace it with an overall sense of ease. Steady is easeful. Try it. Go a little slower. Focus on being at a steady pace. See what happens when you try to force yourself to do something too fast versus being your new turtle self. If you are already slow and steady, focus on being more aware of the moment, relishing the journey and how present you are.

CHAPTER EIGHT

Be Neutral

Tibetan sand mandalas are works of art created to promote peace, healing, and mindfulness for those making them and for those viewing them. The level of intricacy is incredible, and the amount of patience and time required to make one of these is extraordinary. One of the most astounding aspects of these geometric sand images is that once they are completed, they are destroyed. This is to represent the transient nature of everything.

I know what you may be thinking. No, I am not suggesting that once you finish writing whatever it is you are writing you destroy it. What I am saying is that our attachment to what we are writing is what needs to be eliminated. Our attachment is weighing us down. When we are attached to what we have created, there is suffering. With attachments come expectations and pressures that we place on ourselves and our writing. Our attachments then exert a hold on us.

What if that attachment went away? How would we feel?

I experienced this deep form of neutrality when I was writing my memoir. For years, I worked hard writing the first draft. At the same time, I was also trying to survive my mysterious illness. My writing is what kept me going. It was something to focus on. It was something to believe in.

Once my first draft was complete, I set it aside for a few months—as we writers do—to get some much-needed perspective. When I reread the book for what felt like the first time, it was so depressing and dark. *I* didn't even want to read it. If I didn't want to read it, who else would? It defeated the whole purpose of the book.

I made a bold decision. I believed writing my memoir had proven to be a cathartic experience, and I was glad I did it, but I felt it was time to move on, to move forward and not remain in the darkness. I took my manuscript, went down to the local beach, placed the entire book in a pit, and lit it on fire.

Yes.

I burned my book.

For months after that, friends and family would ask me about the progress of my book, and I'd tell them what I did. Everyone was shocked. They tried to convince me to write it again. I didn't want anything to do with it anymore. I believed I had received everything I needed from writing the book, the purging of emotions and deep healing. I was happy to let it go.

About a year later, I had lunch with an old friend, Bob, and he, too, posed the question, "How is the book coming along?" I repeated my story about how I had burned my book. His face held no reaction, and there was a long pause. Finally, he said, "Have you ever read the book *Larry's Kidney*?"

I shook my head.

That was it. He never said another word about it. Strange. I thought I was the crazy one, burning books. Apparently, there was something I was missing.

A few days later, *Larry's Kidney* showed up at my doorstep. The book, not the actual kidney. I read it and realized just how amazing my friend Bob was. The subtitle of the book is *Being the True Story of How I Found Myself in China with My Black Sheep Cousin and His Mail-Order Bride, Skirting the Law to Get Him a Transplant—and Save His Life*.

It was a controversial topic. But the writer knew he needed to inject humor to make it accessible and palatable. My friend knew my story needed levity as well. And he knew I loved humor. A perfect combination.

I took my book (and yes, I had burned the printed pages but had saved an electronic copy, because I may have been sick, but I wasn't an idiot), and I rewrote it with elements of humor. My title even changed from *Undiagnosed* (depressing, right?) to *A Few Minor Adjustments*. My doctor names—and there were many—changed from boring names to protect their privacy, to names that represented the way I viewed them, such as Dr. Loveless, Dr. Nose Hair, Dr. Know-It-All, Dr. Hormone, and Dr. Genius.

Here's the full circle to this story. I love reading. And I feel compelled to give back when I read a book that affects me. I wrote a review for *Larry's Kidney*. Years later, I received an email through my website thanking me for my kind review of a book. It was none other than New York journalist Daniel Asa Rose, author of *Larry's Kidney*. I wrote him back, and I told him the story about how his book influenced me to change mine, which made all the difference. He was flattered. I sent him a copy of my book. Two weeks later, he wrote to say he loved my book and was inspired by my story.

I had to be willing to fully let go of all the work I had done, knowing that my energy and time were not lost. Working on the first version of the book had been meaningful. I also had to let go of what I thought was good and what I thought the book needed. I let time go by and was open to changing things for readers. Because of my willingness to step aside, so many beautiful things happened. Because I was willing to fall, I was willing to be neutral about it and let go of my attachments to what the outcome would be.

The first time I wrote my book was for me. The second version was for the world. This is true of most everything we write. We have a drive and passion, and we want to write. We finish that elusive first draft, yet that is only the beginning. That first draft was for you. You needed to write it, to enjoy the process, to create and share your story and push the boundaries of your imagination. And in some cases, heal. Then, once you are ready, you go back to that story and edit it, rewrite it, slash sentences, sections, even chapters. You are making it ready for the world.

The second time you write the book, it might be vastly different from where it started. That hunk of clay is now sculpted into a striking figure. And you as the writer have changed, too.

My last editor on my memoir—yes, I had multiple editors—instructed me to cut out fourteen polished chapters. I fought with her on this, justifying all I had written. Once I was done feeling shocked, she challenged me to condense the true message of each of those chapters into just one or two sentences at most. I accepted her challenge, believing she would see how important those chapters were. I inserted those few sentences in fitting places throughout the book and deleted the other ninety percent of those chapters. After I completed this exercise, I reread the book.

It was better.

Much better.

Once again, I had to get out of my own way. I had to be open to a more neutral perspective about the whole thing. What a huge difference it made.

As we write, we need to let go and move to a neutral place as much as we can. Create, get it all out, and then let it go.

Know this: You don't have to get rid of your attachments. Keep them if you want to. But there is another way. What if you could be freer without all of it? What if you could give yourself that gift? I am certainly glad I did. And I continue to do it with everything I write.

One of the best ways I can help myself decide whether something stays in a story or not is to ask this single question: Does it serve the story, or does it serve my ego? Honestly answer this question, and you will know whether something stays or goes.

We all have layers of bias and predispositions we can't see. Each time you feel an attachment to something you've written, release it. Remember you are falling. Let it drop. You don't need it. When we are neutral, we glide along unhampered and free.

When another attachment comes up, release that, too. Smile when you do it, and this will invite a sense of freedom. That is what we are moving toward. The more neutral we are, and the more unattached, the more we are free to enjoy the fall.

Keep releasing each new thing that comes up. You will get closer and closer to neutral with each release. Being neutral is a simple concept, one that can take years to truly grasp and embody. It's all about the fall. The more willing you are to let go, the easier it will be. And the more rewarding.

Neutrality doesn't mean indifference—it means being open to what is. Being neutral doesn't mean not having passion. It is the opposite. You can be filled with passion and not be attached to what happens. Be open, and give yourself permission to fully let go. It's okay. Really, it is.

And no, I don't advocate burning books. That was a onetime deal. But I would do it all over again because it was what I needed to do to see this other way.

Also, it's important not to move forward until you have inspiration and clarity. We often artificially set timetables and put pressure on ourselves. Drop the urgency of to-dos, because the best way to destroy your passion is to force yourself to do something out of pressure.

Release that pressure. Know that your writing is there for you to help heal and ease your stress. It is a creative endeavor that will ultimately bring you joy, peace, and transformation. It is always there for you. Take time to write as you can, without pressure. Taking the pressure off will bring you to a lighter place. You'll look forward to the process, and consequently, you'll write more because it enhances your life rather than detracts from it.

Practice & Play

Neutrality isn't an exciting word. Yet, it is important. Being neutral is integral to crafting a story that is best for your audience. What if neutrality is the path to crafting the book you've always wanted to write? Fostering neutrality is a practice that takes time to hone. I struggle with it sometimes, but I keep on, knowing neutrality is required to bring forth the magical stories inside me. Here are some practices to connect to a more neutral place inside you.

PAUSE FOR A POP QUIZ

Think about the piece you are working on. What is your level of attachment to it? Define your level using the scale below. Endeavor to move your score toward 1 as much as you can. It's a practice, so don't worry about being perfect. Just keeping an awareness about where you are will help you become more neutral.

Ready?

1. Neutral—I feel completely neutral about my writing. I am open to feedback and excited to improve my writing. It is a beautiful process, but I am 100% okay with changes and input. It is fine with me if I never finish, and I feel free to let it go at any time.
2. Mildly Attached—I am fairly neutral about my writing. I love the process and want to finish and get published, which would be wonderful. I am open to feedback and excited to improve my writing. Sometimes I feel unsure, but I keep reminding myself of the bigger picture. I am aware of this attachment and am focused on letting it go.

3. Moderately Attached—Yes, I want this story finished and out in the world. I feel a tad anxious about the whole thing. I am somewhat open to feedback, but I get defensive or feel extra sensitive when people give me suggestions about my writing. I am aware of my attachments, and I could possibly let one or two go.
4. Yes, I'm Attached—My story is an important part of me, and writing it is a defining part of my life. I need to write it my way. I am so involved I can't see much else.
5. Absolutely Attached—This is my story/my baby. I'm doing it the way I want, and it is getting out into the world no matter what. I'm the only one who knows what's best for it. Unless you have praise, I don't want your feedback.

SHIFT YOUR ENERGY

Editing is a different energy than writing. You can't be a writer and an editor at the same time. You can do only one. When you write, write. When you edit, edit. When we are editing, we often want that same feeling that initially inspired the writing of that piece. But editing requires a distinct energy that feels different. Instead of editing and revising, lots of people look for something new and ditch the book they are halfway through. This is an opportunity for growth. Notice when you feel like giving up. What emotions are coming up around your project? Emotions are like weather. They come and go. We don't want to add to them, but we don't want to ignore them either. Feel them, and let them go, and head back to neutral again. Keep noticing and being an observer. Bring a sense of wonder and humor to it all. This will shift your energy and the energy of your writing and your editing.

BALANCE

When we overedit, revising something over and over again, there is a perfectionistic quality to it that can prohibit us from moving forward. Why are we compelled to do this? Are we making it better, or are we afraid to move on? Do we feel we will be judged if it isn't perfect? How can we learn to let go of perfection and enjoy the journey? Editing and revising are beneficial and necessary, but there can be too much. Why are you editing? Is it because you know it needs it and you feel right doing it, or are you doing it from a place of fear about being inadequate? Once there is balance, you can build. Balance is fundamental. If you do not have balance, whatever you build on top of it will tumble down.

WELCOME NEUTRALITY

We can't control most things in life—even though our mind tries to tell us otherwise. The more we try to control our writing, the more we will be attached. Here are some inquiries to ask yourself about your current project. Be as open and honest as you can. This is intended to help you see where you are with what you are writing.

1. If everyone—yes, everyone—were to read my story, would I still write it? (Yes, everyone. Even those who may judge you.) Why?
2. If no one were to read my story, would I still write it? Why?

PART THREE

Intuition

The power has always been within you.

CHAPTER NINE

Be a Genius

I doubt that anyone in the history of the history of all history would dispute that Albert Einstein was a genius. He was indeed in every sense of the word.

Yes, I'm asking you to be a genius. To be like Einstein. Simple, right?

It seems like an impossible climb.

It's not.

I'm not saying we'll all be able to solve the world's most complex equations after reading this chapter. But you can tap into your own creative genius, just like Einstein, crazy hair and all (this part is optional).

Einstein was a genius, but he was also a proponent of all the "I" words that I absolutely love and feel are important for us as creative beings. He attributed his discoveries not to knowledge and intellect but to these "I" words. What are these magical words? Coincidentally (not really, but hey), they are the same as the four parts of this book: Inspiration, Innovation, Intuition, and Imagination.

We've already spoken about the first two of these. It's time for intuition.

There is a wonderful quote attributed to Einstein that says it best: "I think ninety-nine times and find nothing. I stop thinking, swim in silence, and the truth comes to me."

What exactly is intuition? It's having a profound trust in something and knowing it to be true. We writers are in our heads way too much. But great writing doesn't come from the mind; it comes from this other place. It comes from a *feeling* place. We are being asked to trust, to observe the mind, and, instead of letting it take over or interfere, to watch and allow our inner knowing to lead.

Intuition resides in this quiet space where we can free ourselves of the constraints of our minds. Intuition is not about logical deduction but about following your inner knowing. This inner guide is your most valuable writing tool. It will help you to know what is best for your story and for you. Fear and limiting thoughts are formed in your mind and from your ego. Intuition is supportive, free, and flowing, not critical or scary.

Our minds are feral. They are all over the place and usually anchored in negative emotions. This is because the mind is focused on one thing: survival. Instead of trying to control the mind, we can remind the mind that we are safe. We can set the mind aside, which makes space for our creative genius to come out and play. Intelligence flows from intuition and creativity. Your mind may be active, but your intuition is more expansive. There are so many possibilities when we tap into our intuition.

The mind gets caught up in worries of the past and future, which is not helpful. It fears losing control. The mind likes logic and reason because it controls through logic and reason. Intuition is always in the present moment. When we listen to our intuition and our heart's desires, we are creating from a more pure and open space. Like with falling, we can take time to look around and enjoy the experience instead of trying to think our way out of it.

One of my favorite clients is a guy who was writing a book about all his years as a theater actor. He has written plays (he even adapted one of Ray Bradbury's plays and got to spend opening night with him) and has a solid command of words. However, his confidence waned when it came to writing a book. When he approached me for help, his ideas were jumbled, the manuscript was super long (almost twice the standard length for that type of book), and it had all the normal hiccups I see in many first drafts.

What I also saw was his genius.

He is a great playwright. He had written one scene in the book like he was writing a play, with the scene setup, setting, and dialogue. And it worked. With some tweaking, it could be a powerful device. I asked him about it, and he was a little embarrassed, as if it was a mistake to put it in. "Maybe I should take it out?"

"On the contrary," I said. "You are a thespian and playwright, and that is why people will be drawn to your book. Why not play to your strengths? I'd like to see this throughout your book. It'll show us even more of who you are. This is your brilliance."

He trusted me and, more importantly, he learned to trust his instincts, the reason he included that piece in the first place. After several drafts and lots of inspired writing, his book worked beautifully. All I could think to say when it came out was, "Bravo!"

In the beginning when I work with a writer, I get paid to read and edit their book. After all our time working together, the most remarkable thing happens. I witness writers tapping into their genius by following their intuition—I would now *pay* to read their book.

Get comfortable not listening to your mind. It can be a challenge, as we are used to obeying it. One way to do this is to look more closely at your words. What energy do they have? Are they positive, flowing, and joyful, or are they stifled and riddled with anxiety, doubt, and fear? Look for the goose bumps. You know, those moments when everything clicks and feels right or you have this amazing idea and you can't type fast enough to get it all on to the page. That's when you are truly in tune with your intuition.

We can't control the thoughts that surface in our minds. But we can change our perception of them, and our experiences will change based on that shift. The mind isn't the villain; it's trying to help us. But the mind is reactionary. That's why Einstein talked about swimming in silence. When he quieted his mind, his breakthroughs had room to grow. He could employ his mind to work toward those discoveries.

You can do the same.

Don't let the mind take you somewhere you don't want to go, or worse, stop you from starting at all. Don't sacrifice your joy on the inside for something you are working toward on the outside that doesn't align with what you really want. That is the mind talking. When you notice these things happening, thank the mind, acknowledge its presence, and then ask it to step aside and be quiet. You've got important intuitive business to attend to—like falling.

Practice & Play

Being a genius is just as much about intellect as it is about getting in touch with your intuition. Be willing to be led by your intuition. It can be insightful and also fun. Trusting your intuition takes some getting used to, but it is worth it. Here are a few practices to help you along. Find what works for you, and explore the infinite possibilities of play available in the realms of intuition.

TRUST

The first ingredient to being more in tune with your intuition is trust. By cultivating trust, you can make better choices that support your unique and most authentic perspective as a writer. Practice making choices from a feeling place, not a thinking place. Here's how. Before you make a choice on any aspect of your writing journey, ask yourself these questions:

- Does this decision fill me up? Inspire me? Bring me joy? Is it fun? Is it fulfilling?

OR

- Does it bring me down? Detract from my purpose? Drain my energy? Feel awkward? Or unfulfilling?

DIG DEEP

There may be times when you can't get your mind to stop thinking. That's okay. Remember, it's normal for the mind to produce thoughts. That's what it is supposed to do. Just be aware of this. You can follow your thoughts and look deeper into what is being communicated. With awareness comes freedom. Use these inquiries to practice tapping into your intuition and to see what is blocking you from being fully engaged with it.

- What is my mind telling me that isn't true?
- What external influences are blocking or drowning out my inner wisdom?
- What physical sensations accompany my intuitive insights and inner knowing?
- What can I learn from the times I ignored or did not trust my intuition?
- What do I need to trust my deeper wisdom?

Take some time with your answers. Observe any patterns, and identify any specifics that you can work through, such as fears or anxieties that may be impacting your confidence. Think about practical ways to incorporate quiet time into your daily writing routine. Practice journaling, perhaps meditation, or spending time in nature to enhance your intuitive skills. The more you practice listening to your intuition, the more familiar following it will feel when you go to write.

FEEL IT

Brilliant writers are exceptional not because they tried to fit in or stand out. They got that way because they went within. They trusted and followed their intuition and passion. Following is a practice to help you discover your inner knowing and biggest passions. When doing this practice, stay out of your logical mind. Write from your instincts and how you feel. This will help you see different correlations with your writing path by staying out of the mind and tapping into a deeper place.

- Think of two or three books you've read that have changed your life. Pick one.
- Write about how it impacted you. How did it make you feel?
- What did it prompt you to do? How did it get you to look at your life differently?
- Did it inspire you to write?
- Now, think of the story/book you are writing. Why did you choose to write in that genre? Why are you writing that story?
- How does writing your story feel to you?
- Are there any parallels between the book you chose and your story? What can you learn from this?

Knowing these answers can help sculpt your writing and hone your craft to be more aligned with your deeper purpose. You can bring this knowledge to the page, infusing it throughout your story and creating a more meaningful piece for you and your audience.

WRITE IN WHITE

There are many ways to get out of our heads when we are writing. One of my favorites is to write in white. Change your font color on your computer from black to white. Then type away. You won't be able to see what you are typing, because the letters are white and match the background of the page. But you can trust they are there. This frees you to focus on the creative energy coming through and not judge or edit as you go. Then, when you are finished with that page, paragraph, chapter, or writing session, you can switch the font back to black and revise and edit as needed. If handwriting, purchase an invisible ink pen, which is fantastic for shorter projects and stream of consciousness or journal writing. The ink is invisible, but the cap has a nifty light that you can shine on the ink to see what is there. I don't recommend these pens for an entire book, but they are worthwhile tools to use from time to time to help free you from your thoughts.

CHAPTER TEN

Be Playful

As much as I adore reading, I also delight in watching a well-crafted movie. The most memorable and powerful movies have three things in common: an imaginative idea, a meaningful message, and a top-notch script. Yes, the acting, directing, editing, cinematography, costume design, etc. are essential, but without these three fundamentals, the story wouldn't connect with anyone.

A little secret—some of my favorite movies are animated. Why? Because they have an infinite amount of room to be creative and aren't constrained by the laws of physics or our humanness. And most of the time, they have all three of the essentials I mentioned.

These movies are also some of my favorites because they embody playfulness, one of the key ingredients of being a writer. Play!

The world is our playground. Somewhere along the way we've forgotten this. Adults laugh three to five times a day, while children laugh three to four hundred times. Children aren't trying to make themselves laugh; it comes from play. When we play, we are truly living in the moment. We are present. With a shift of perspective and willingness to be silly and spontaneous, we can find joy in everything, even in what may seem negative.

Am I saying we all need to be more like children and animated characters? Why yes—yes, I am. Especially animated characters because they ooze positivity in the face of so much upheaval. They are often falling. It's bedlam. But they enjoy the ride.

When we write, we have a choice in how we show up. We can be negative, stressed, worried, attached, and trying to force something. Or we can be happy, with the belief that everything is going to turn out all right. We can be positive, playful, and untroubled when things don't go the way we envisioned. Our focus is on playing and having some laughs along the way. And if it turns out we craft a piece that achieves more—entertains, informs, inspires, motivates, transforms, and reaches people—wonderful. There is more of a chance this will happen when we enjoy the journey.

I recently met a science fiction writer at a conference I was working at. It was her first conference and her first book. We had a one-on-one consultation to discuss her submitted pages. Her story was engaging, the writing flowed well, and I was hooked to see what happened. I gave her my feedback for some improvements, and about six weeks later she called me and wanted me to edit her whole manuscript, saying how much my feedback resonated with her. I was delighted to help.

"How long is your manuscript?"

"About 117,000 words."

"Great."

"Yeah, I like the length, and it only took me about three months to write."

Whoa.

I paused. Took a moment to consider this. When I hear that someone has written a book in that short of time, I get a little concerned about the quality. That the writer rushed through it or did that "Write Your Book in Just One Month" contest and now believes the book is ready to publish. But I had seen the first twenty-five pages of her book and her detailed outline. At least from my limited vantage point, I could see that the attention to detail and writing quality were there.

"How did you write this so fast?" I asked, curious what her secret was, and she gave me her answer:

> I had this story brewing in me for a couple years. I kept thinking about it, dreaming about it. It wouldn't leave me alone. It was interrupting my life. So, I finally sat down and said, *Okay, just write.* Then, it was like a gigantic download. I couldn't stop myself. I just had to keep going until it was all out of me. And I had such a good time doing it. I realized I was doing what I most loved. And it felt easy. Not like work at all. Only fun.

I smiled, feeling as though I understood exactly what she meant. Follow your joy, and you will move mountains, or pages and pages of writing.

Yes, she had good overall writing skills, but she had the most important element: joy. She loved writing her story, the world she was building, and it showed not only in her writing but also in the way she talked about it. She exuded happiness. She was committed to the joy, not to a chore, a should, a hurdle, or a challenge. And this will assuredly make all the difference for her.

If we are not having fun, why are we writing? Doing it to get it done isn't a recipe for inspired prose. When we rediscover the art of playing, our words, our process, and our messages come alive.

This doesn't mean writing isn't challenging. Think of it this way. Have you ever done something difficult, but you had so much passion for it, as tough as it was, you still wanted to do it because it brought you joy?

Exactly.

Make choices that support your passion in writing. By focusing on the fun, you will be uplifted and led to something joyful and amazing.

Practice & Play

Writing is a privilege and a beautiful endeavor. We get to take something from inside and share it with our friends and family, the world, our pets … maybe even a sea otter or two. Before those words can be ready for others, we need to go through the journey of creation. Why not make it fun? Most of us have veered off track, away from our childlike essence. We need to rediscover this innate part of ourselves. At first, it can feel like trudging through mud. Be patient and practice. The more time you practice, the more natural and freeing it will feel. Once you master this playful approach, you'll never want to go back. There are an infinite number of ways you can bring joy to being a writer. Here are a few to propel you in that direction.

GIVE YOURSELF PERMISSION

It is important to give ourselves permission to play when we write. As adults, we tend to be shy about being playful, especially when so much turmoil exists in the world. When we play, we raise our energy. The more we live in joy, the more joy we can share. More joy will be reflected in our writing. Give yourself permission to explore all the realms of your playful self. Enjoy the process. Write to these inquiries, and see if you can extract the joy of being a writer.

- What is joyful about my writing process?
- What is joyful about this piece I am writing?
- How can I make my writing more playful?
- What doesn't feel fun about being a writer?
- How can I shift my perspective to be more like a playful kid?

EXPRESS THROUGH ART

Being a writer is having more than a superficial desire to produce something. There is a deeper yearning, a passion to create. Let's be with our words in a new way to spark some playfulness. Take a large, blank piece of paper or canvas. Grab some markers, colored pencils, or paints, and create something inspired from what you are writing. Don't worry; it will not end up in the Louvre Museum. If it does, maybe instead of writing, you might want to consider painting. But here is the point: No one else but you need see it. This is about bringing passion back to your story. Let your imagination flow. You can draw your characters; write out your theme or message in fantastic fonts, shapes, and colors; or write passages in interesting ways. Whatever you do, let it come from an uninhibited place. Connect with your writing and your project, and find the joy of why you started writing in the first place. You can do this multiple times for different scenes or characters or for any number of aspects of your writing. For those who want to take it a notch further, draw or create with your nondominant hand. This will free your logical mind and bring you more into playfulness since you will be more engaged with the colors and lines than the technique you execute.

RELEASE JUDGMENT

We can't enjoy something if we are judgmental about it. Once you start judging, you are disconnected from joy. When you release your judgments, you can delight in feeling boundless as you plunge into what you are creating. Letting go of judgment is not a single decision—it's an ongoing practice. Deeply ingrained habits of self-criticism or doubt don't disappear overnight. Be patient with yourself and notice when judgment arises. Instead of resisting or suppressing it, acknowledge it with curiosity. What does it want to protect you from? What assumptions is it based on? To help this process along, cultivate self-compassion. Treat your inner critic like a worried friend—listen, but don't let it dictate your creative choices. To help you be more at ease and playful, explore answers to the following inquiries:

- What judgments do I have about being a writer?
- What judgments do I have about *what* I am writing?
- How would I feel if I could drop these judgments?
- What would help me let go of these judgments?

Maybe if we stop judging ourselves and our process, and stop trying so hard, we could have a bit more fun. Just for one day, give up judging and trying and simply be with the flow of playfulness. See what happens.

MOVE

Movement sparks vitality. Movement also releases stagnant energy. Have fun exploring different ways you can move to enhance your writing. Dance, skip, jump, stretch, roll, and bounce your way to feeling more positive and freer to create. Take just five minutes to move about before you write or during a break from your writing session. By incorporating even gentle movement, you can increase your energy, relax your body, and clear your mind. I like to go for a walk in nature, Hula-Hoop, dance to songs on my "Happy" playlist, or bounce up and down on my yoga ball. All these give me that extra boost and get me excited about my writing.

CHAPTER ELEVEN

Be Friends with Fear

I don't believe in writer's block.

You may be shaking your head and wanting to shout, "It's real. I experience it all the time." I hear you. I do. I have felt those feelings many times until I figured out what was beneath them. Then I was free.

There is nothing blocking us, per se. We arrive at a place that feels like a block from our words because of lack of inspiration or fear.

If we are not feeling inspired, passionate, or interested, it's challenging to create. It can feel like something is stacked up against us. But when we have a zest for the subject we are writing about or the project we are working on, we feel ease and joy. As described in Part 1, we need to proactively foster our inspiration every day to keep our writing life flowing. That means finding activities, places, and people that elevate us, raise our energy, and bring us to new possibilities. This will bring the magic back to writing.

Now, let's look at that other fun subject called fear.

For me it *is* a fun topic. I've spent a lot of my life with fears, and I have learned so much from them. I love talking about fear because with openness and willingness, we can transcend our fears and embody a different relationship with them. This gigantic fall leads us to true freedom.

Lots of people talk about facing fears, which can be confrontational. Not me. I believe in befriending fears since they have a lot to teach us. Fears are here to show us something, to help us, not to hurt us. The more we suppress, ignore, or neglect them, the more powerful they become. Here's an example that was one of my first real lessons in being with fear in a different way.

I was writing my memoir, and lots of scary stuff was coming up. My writing mentor, Matt, who is a shamanic explorer and badass in many ways, guided me throughout my journey. One day, I approached him with what wasn't a writing dilemma but something that was blocking my creative energy. I was having night terrors. Every night for weeks. They were all about the same thing.

The *Poltergeist* clown.

I don't have a problem with clowns. Except for this one. Ever since I was a kid, this fictitious being bothered me. During this writing project, it kept showing up in my sleep states, freaking me out and causing me to wake up sweating and screaming.

For months this went on. Then, a serendipitous event pushed me over the edge. I went to visit my father in Vegas. He took me to lunch at Planet Hollywood, which has American fare and lots of movie memorabilia. It was a ninety-minute wait to be seated. In the hot afternoon sun, we paced, and our hunger grew.

Finally, they called our name, and the host led us to our table. As I slid into the cheap red vinyl-cushioned booth, I stopped. Directly across from us in a glass case, no more than ten feet away was, you guessed it, in all its glory, the original *Poltergeist* clown.

I begged the host for another table. There wasn't one.

I now had to have lunch with my worst nightmare. I would like to say that I resolved something in those two hours (the restaurant was packed and the service painfully slow), but no. I almost ran out screaming every other minute. And I swear that clown kept eyeing my onion rings.

A week later, my nightmares became more intense. I called Matt. I told him what had been happening and about my latest surprise rendezvous with the evil puppet.

Matt's scratchy, deep voice reached a crescendo. "Aww. I get it. You know what you need to do?"

"No. If I did, I would have done it already."

"Ah, that's what you think."

Confused, I waited for more.

"It's not that easy. And most people don't want to do it."

"What?"

"Have you ever asked the clown what it wants?"

My mouth opened to speak, but nothing came out.

His voice came through more animated and powerful. "You gotta talk to it. See what it wants. Your fears, they want something from you. You gotta figure that out. The only way is to go deeper into the terror. Then you'll get your answers. If you don't, it will keep coming for you. And then that lunch you had will look like a jolly picnic."

That night, I set up a plan. I told myself that when the clown came lunging at me with all the horror in its eyes and those long, thin red-and-white striped arms trying to strangle me, I would stand still and ask the question. Not from a threatening place, or from a stance of trying to overcome my fear, but from a place of calm and curiosity.

The nightmare happened as planned, and in a lucid moment, I stood strong and peaceful and asked, "What do you want? Is there something you need from me?"

The clown stopped a few inches from me, looked into my eyes, and smiled. Not his normal, wicked smile, but a sheepish grin of someone misunderstood. Then he spoke. "I just want you to see me. That's all I've ever wanted."

I remembered all the years I couldn't look at him, or I ran away, or I hid. Like all of us in this life, we want to be seen, heard, and appreciated for whatever and whoever we are. Even the unsavory parts of ourselves. Even the malicious clown part.

I smiled back at him. "I see you. I'm sorry I was too scared to before."

The clown flashed a brilliant smile and disappeared like particles evaporating. That was the last time I ever saw him.

There are many ways to interpret this story. For me, it meant I needed to not be afraid of what I was scared of. Sounds crazy. But it was a profound shift in my writing and in my life.

Within a week, I was writing in full force again, no longer afraid of exposing all those dark corners of myself I didn't want to see. I gave myself the gift of owning the totality of myself as a writer and human being. And I loved all of it.

What fears are holding you back from being truly free when you write? And from being free in your life? Writing and life are intertwined. Amazing writing happens when we are willing to embrace what our fears are trying to show us. Same with life.

Writing can be a challenging experience because lots of feelings and pent-up emotions that have been hiding for who-knows-how-long can come up. Especially when we are writing about heavy topics. We need to learn to get comfortable with being uncomfortable. This can be healing. Especially when it comes to writing memoirs. Memoirs are mirrors. Mirrors are monsters waiting to be seen and loved. If you don't write memoir, think again. Everything we write is part memoir. It's us. It's who we are, wanting to be seen and understood. Before other people can hear, see, appreciate, and understand us and what we are conveying, we must hear, see, appreciate, and understand ourselves.

How can you befriend your fears? To befriend fear is to make a conscious shift—from resistance to acceptance. It means noticing the tight grip fear has on your voice, your flow, and your self-expression—and gently loosening that grip, not by pushing harder but by softening into it. Instead of resisting the fall—the moments when inspiration dips, when self-doubt creeps in—what if you welcomed it? What if you loved the fall for the clarity it brings, for the honesty it demands, for the healing and transformation? Love it for what it is giving you. This will bring you that freedom you long for in writing and in life.

When we stop resisting, we stop giving fear power over us. This is how freedom happens. Not in waiting for the fear to go away but in choosing to move forward with it, embracing it and the full experience we are having. Then, our writing becomes more truthful, alive, and resonant.

Trust is a big component when it comes to being with our fears. It's about trusting something beyond your control. Fear cannot live in you when you have profound trust or when you feel complete acceptance and love for something or someone.

I say, love your fears. Because in reality, everything is love. Let me explain.

A writer friend of mine writes romance and teaches at some of the same conferences I do. His sessions are wildly popular, and they are usually at the same time as mine (a running joke we have since we can't ever attend each other's sessions). One year, I managed to sit in on one of his talks called, "Every Story Is a Love Story." His premise for the workshop was that every book and every movie ever made comes back to the theme of love. Every single one.

Think about it.

Pride and Prejudice. Easy. Romantic love.

Tuesdays with Morrie. Yes. Love for a mentor.

The Hunger Games. Uh-huh. Love between sisters.

Harry Potter. Definitely. Love for his friends and parents and Hogwarts.

The Lord of the Rings. Absolutely. Love between best friends Frodo and Sam.

Jaws. Yup. Chief Brody's love for the town and the people and the safety of his family.

And yes, even *Poltergeist*. A family's love to survive and save one another.

I could keep going, but I think you get the point.

If every story is about love, then our writing stems from that place, too. Writing is being with all our fears and coming back to love. It's about loving ourselves enough to dig deep, find out what is in our way, and dive into the depths to free whatever needs help. Sometimes we will have major challenges that take more than asking one simple question to resolve. In these cases, seek support from professionals, family, and friends. But know this. It's worth it to get to the other side.

Practice & Play

Have you ever heard the saying, "Everyone loves the warmth of the fire, but no one wants to get burned"? We all love the ups of the writing life. Those highs, the striking blaze that keeps us warm and fills us up. But most of us want to avoid the dark places. I invite you to see all sides of the fire, the beauty and the beast, if you will. Both are magnificent.

MAKE NEW FRIENDS

Let's make friends with your writing fears. It's okay. We all have them. I've got a long list that I've worked through. Ask yourself these two questions and be as honest and open to receiving answers as you can.

- What is my biggest challenge in writing?
- What is my biggest fear in writing?

Get support from loved ones as you delve into these. Write as much as you can about each one, allowing a free flow of everything that needs to surface to be heard, felt, and then released. When you are finished, let these go by ripping them up, shredding them, or safely burning them.

ACKNOWLEDGE YOUR INNER CRITIC

As writers, the inner critic can feel like a constant shadow, questioning every word, doubting every idea. But what if, instead of fighting it, you simply acknowledged it? And then what if you set it free? Notice its voice, thank it for trying to protect you, and then gently release it. You don't need perfection—you need presence. Trust the part of you that longs to express, not impress. That's where your true voice lives. Let your words come forth with no filter, no judgments. Allow them to come from the purest space within you. Anytime a judgment comes in, notice it, and let it pass by. The ego and the mind want to keep you stuck in fear. You can free yourself by not engaging or giving power to your inner critic. You have a choice to give power to the critic or to the place in you that ignites joy. What do you choose?

RIDE THE WAVES

We writers are all over the map emotionally. One minute, we are the next J. K. Rowling, Chimamanda Ngozi Adichie, Keats, Toni Morrison, Hemingway, or Shakespeare (pick your person). Or we are even better. The next moment, we are awful, the worst writer who ever typed a word. These are the ups and downs of a writer's life. We allow our mind to take us for a ride. In reality, the waves of creation are simply roaring up and down. See if you can stop feeding those doubts, anxieties, and fears. Thank them and go back to the joy.

You are not the greatest writer to ever be, and you are certainly not the worst. We all are different and have varied abilities, preferences, education, understanding, and levels of talent. The best and worst are nothing but fallacies. If you write, then you are a creative being with something to offer. Ride the waves of these ups and downs pulsing inside you. Know they will come and go. They do not define you. When a big wave hits, see if you can get a little excited since this is a big moment for transformation waiting and ready to happen. Listen solely to the love emanating from within, to that passion directing you toward your newest creation. It's the voice that speaks the truth. Remember, the waves are what move you forward.

EMBRACE YOUR HERO'S JOURNEY

It's probably taken a lot to reach where you are in life. Don't stop here. Keep going. Look within yourself and see how you can open yourself up to this grand adventure of writing and all it can bestow upon you. You have the power. You are living your own hero's journey. Take time and answer these inquiries to see what's inside you waiting to be seen. Notice what comes up for you. Know that there is fuel in your fears that can be alchemized for the higher good of your life and your writing.

- What is keeping me from being my truest self when I write?
- What is keeping me from reaching my highest and best potential?
- What am I afraid of?

Once you've answered these inquiries, try some affirming statements to help you change the language of your mind to shift to a higher, more loving tone.

- I am on my own hero's journey.
- I have a unique voice, and I am ready to be heard.
- My story is worthwhile and meaningful.
- I am worthwhile and meaningful.
- I love all of me, and I am ready to be seen.

CHAPTER TWELVE

Believe

If you've been playing along, you are now fully present in each moment, clear about your why, regularly inspired, and you know the power of being intentional. You are always curious, willing to be guided by surprise, completely neutral about everything, and you act like a turtle. You are also a creative genius who shows up in this world as a jovial, animated character who skips down the street hand in hand with your fears.

Not much to it.

What's missing?

Let me tell you a story. I hope my memory serves me right since this is a story about a story. Here is what I recall.

I was at a writers' conference, one of my favorite events of the year. The evening speaker was a talented and famous writer. She stepped onto the stage and addressed the audience from behind the lectern. Her bright yellow top and golden hair were radiant, matching her magnetic smile. She spoke with such joy. "You can't imagine what this conference meant to me. If it had not been for this conference, I'd probably still be on a rerun of a game show somewhere."

We all laughed.

Then, she told us why.

Every year at this conference, awards are offered for fiction, nonfiction, and poetry. There is also an award given for the best writing on a topic such as "When we last met." At the conference years ago, she was nervous for others to read her words, but she entered the competition for the topic award.

She won.

She read her winning story aloud to the room of writers. Afterward, the director of the conference said something to the effect of, "You've got a real talent. A natural storyteller. You should keep writing and do something with this."

She stammered, then said, "I can't."

"Why not?"

The story she had submitted was written from the perspective of a child and written the way a child would write. "This is the way I really write," she told the director. "I am dyslexic. I can't spell, and I'm horrible with grammar."

Without hesitation, the director said, "Oh, honey, that's what editors are for."

Before this moment, she had been a brilliant actor and comedienne. After, she went on to fulfill her dream of being an author. She has written several more books, has been nominated for an Academy Award for Best Adapted Screenplay, and is a winner of the Harper Lee Award.

What she needed was to believe in herself. By putting herself out there and being vulnerable, both in submitting her story and in sharing her challenges, she was able to move past them, do what she loved, and not let her perceived limitations stop her.

After her talk, I rushed to buy her newest book and to meet her. She was as lovely in person as I had imagined.

We don't often realize how our long-held, limiting beliefs prevent us from moving forward. It can feel challenging to let go of them when they are so ingrained. What if we tried? What if, like this author, we put ourselves out there and believed?

It doesn't matter what anyone else is thinking or saying. It only matters what you believe. If *you* don't believe, it will never happen. Believing in yourself changes everything.

It is also important to surround yourself with people who support and believe in you. They can help you see what you are not able to see. This can make all the difference.

Here's something else to consider. Your past is not the path.

This line came to me one evening when I was taking a bath. I didn't have a pen or device anywhere near to write it down. My relaxing bath became a battle against forgetting.

After thirty minutes of repeating this like a mantra and thinking about the truth behind it, I began to see the bigger picture. So now, each time I start wandering into yesterday (like when I hear that Beatles song), I remind myself that what I am seeking is right here, right now (Jesus Jones, you sang it well).

What are you holding on to? Are you aligning with your past or your future? Align with who you are now and what dreams you have. Who you think you were and where you have been do not matter. What is important is who you are now and where you want to go moving forward. It's time to let go of the past. Thank it and be happy for all you experienced. Focusing on it will keep you stuck there. The more you let go, the more space you have for new opportunities to emerge. And the more you'll grow.

What is keeping you from believing in yourself? What is standing in your way?

Be aware of your beliefs. Bring them to the surface. Ask yourself what beliefs are keeping you from starting, finishing, or continuing your writing.

If we look at some of the discourse in our society about writing, it is no wonder we all view writing as a difficult and tiresome activity. Some of the most masterful writers have said writing is a painful, exhausting endeavor. It's hard, arduous, and full of doubt and struggle. Because of this, it is hard to believe in ourselves.

I believe there is another way. Writing is what you say it is. If you think writing is hard, then chances are, it will be. If you think it is easy, then it will be.

What if writing a book were easy?

And fun?

It can be.

We first need to believe. Then, what we believe can become our reality. Taking it a step further, we have to believe what we believe in. I know that may sound silly, but it's all about having profound trust—an inherent knowing and belief that you have everything in you to get wherever you want to go.

In other words, the power you are seeking lies within you. All writing is from within you. Nothing happens outside you or to you. The writing experience is from the inside. The outside will never happen exactly the way you want, but the inside can. Give yourself this gift of believing. Go inside yourself and find the honest, core feelings that light you up.

Belief is not about thinking or trying to force something. It is being with a truth that resides deep within you. Be patient and gentle with yourself as you explore what is happening inside you. Most of all, be playful. Writing is an art, a sincere joy, and a privilege. We don't *have* to write. We *get* to write.

Adults, on average, make around thirty-five thousand decisions a day. How do we know we are making the right decisions when it comes to being a writer? It's easy. Show up and write. Do it for the joy and the passion and because you can't imagine doing anything else. Believe in yourself, and the rest will follow.

Practice & Play

Belief is a necessity for writers and for life. Hope is helpful, but it still keeps us longing for or wanting a future that may never happen. We hope for something, and this is often on shaky ground. Belief is knowing. We realize something within ourselves, and we shift to a state of certainty and all the confidence and acceptance that go along with it. We start to feel what it will be like when what we believe in comes true. Here are some practices to help you arrive at the beautiful place of believing in yourself.

TAKE A QUANTUM LEAP

Being a writer is often about committing to something you can't quite grasp yet. Taking that leap into the unknown. Believing. How we experience writing is a direct reflection of the way we perceive our reality. Are you willing to take that leap? Do you believe in yourself? If yes, excellent! Why? If not, why? What is in your way? What is it you know and feel about your writing journey? Take time with these inquiries and make that quantum leap from hope to belief.

LISTEN AND BE

This practice is about quieting our minds and being with what is inside us, wanting to be heard. Find some quiet time, away from all distractions and your electronic devices. You don't need a pen or paper for this practice. Sit comfortably. Set an intention for hearing what wants to come to the surface and be heard. What is it you need to know? What is it that you believe? Once you are clear on what you would like to know, set a timer for five to ten minutes. Then simply be. Don't do anything. Be a patient observer of what your inner voice is saying. Listen without judgment. Then, once the timer dings, reflect upon your experience. What did you learn? Now you can write about it, if you wish.

FREE YOURSELF FROM LIMITING BELIEFS

Are you ready to release your past? It's not always easy. Letting go can stir up fear, doubt, shame, or even grief. But beneath these feelings is freedom. The freedom to write, express, and simply be without old stories holding you back.

Begin by asking yourself, What are some limiting beliefs I have been carrying? Maybe it's "I'm not good enough" or "No one will care what I have to say." Write them all down. Be honest and be tender with yourself. This is not about judging yourself but about cultivating awareness and compassion. Pause and take a breath. Notice how you feel and what comes up for you. Sadness? Resistance? Shame? Anger? Frustration? They are all okay. These feelings are part of the process. Acknowledge them.

Next, ask yourself, What would help me release these beliefs? A daily affirmation or reminder from your higher self? A talk with your best friend? Listening to your favorite song? Going out in nature and breathing in fresh air? Write these down, too. They are part of your writer's tool kit.

Lastly, when you are finished, take your list of limiting beliefs and release them. Either rip the paper or burn it safely. But let them all go. As you do this, say, "Thank you for everything you taught me. I'm ready to say goodbye to the past and hello to the beautiful blank page waiting for me."

Remember, the blank page is not an empty space or source of stress; it is an open invitation to create. It is full of possibility. It is a gift, and it is waiting for you to believe.

PAUSE

Instead of rushing to fill the page with words, take time to pause and listen. Writing is not just about creating but also about receiving the inspiration that already exists around and within you. When you embrace stillness, you invite ideas to surface naturally, without forcing them. Cultivate the art of patience in your writing process. Trust that the words will come when you give space to your thoughts and creativity. Ask yourself: What feels ready to emerge? and remind yourself, "I am a conduit for stories that are meant to be told." This practice helps you write with greater ease and feel more connected to your creative flow. To help you along, you can also use the following affirmation: "Writing is my playground. I grow every time I write." Shifting your point of view to slow down and notice the joys and the opportunities that await you will help you pause so you can appreciate the fall.

PART FOUR
Imagination

Imagine all that is possible.

It's ALL possible.

CHAPTER THIRTEEN

Be Part of the Three C's

Imagine ...

One of my favorite words. This word is an invitation, a directive, a possibility, a living poem. It is strong and gives us license to play, stands fierce and gentle, and is our entry point into creation.

What we add to this word "imagine" and where we go from there is our choice. Sometimes it can feel daunting to have limitless portals to explore. Yet if we open ourselves up and stand in the center of this opportunity, uninhibited and free, we can soar.

John Lennon daringly asked the world to imagine a place different from the one we were living in, a place of harmony and peace. What a powerful vision. Every time I hear that song, "Imagine," I feel connected to something bigger than my tiny life on this tiny planet in this expansive universe. It reminds me peace is possible. That borders, boundaries, and limitations of our fearful minds can be transmuted. And I know I am not the only one.

Lennon imagined and created, and then he shared. From this, we all received the gift of connection. We are connected to a profound idea captured in a beautiful work of art. We are also connected to something we can believe in. It all started from one person's imagination.

As writers, we have this great power available to us at any time. We simply need to go there. When we do, we become a part of what I call "The Three C's of Being a Writer." These C's are a wondrous place to be.

I already mentioned the first C, Connection. Words can bridge the gaps in our humanity, bringing us together through our triumphs and pains and our grace. We can swim in each other's thoughts and feel the profundity of our individual, earthly sojourns while exploring the deep emotional landscape of our hearts. In essence, words connect us. As writers, we get the honor of building these bridges in a multitude of ways.

We get to share our gifts, imagination, and big ideas with the world. Our creations need not sit unseen and lonely in our desk drawer, or on some hidden, password-protected file on our computer. Of course, we can choose to simply write for our own passion and fulfillment. Not everything is meant to be shared. And that sole act of creation is enough on its own. But there is also a magnificent beauty in taking the next step—contributing to the world. One of the most beautiful aspects of writing is bypassing the small talk and surface-level conversations. We dive straight to the heart of who we are, what we are pondering, and what we want to really say. We break through the noise and form bonds with others who are seeking ways to leap forward in their own lives. Connection is one of the main reasons we write—we connect with ourselves and the world, and we foster relationships.

The second C is Community. Being part of a group of people who get you is like having access to oxygen. It's essential to survival. Writing is often a secluded activity, and even the most introverted writers need to come up for air, talk shop, and get feedback from others who understand.

The writing community can be incredible. Within a few minutes of meeting another writer, we can passionately explore for hours the inner workings of our latest creations. We can brainstorm something we are struggling with, and another writer will offer a brilliant solution to something that has eluded us for six months. We discuss the process, the flow, the anxieties and struggles, and the joys and bright spots. We go deep. We give suggestions to elevate another's prose, and we receive clarity on things we couldn't see on our own. We reach within and give our time, energy, and talent to help strangers keep moving forward with their journey. Those strangers do the same for us.

These are our people.

A perfect example of the power of community just occurred yesterday. I meditate daily, and I belong to many groups that focus on meditation and healing. I met this guy, and we were messaging about some of the challenges and traumas that led us to our current way of seeing the world and living. He knew I was a writer, and here's what he wrote to me:

> I'm a hobbyist writer. I did get some good feedback from agents, but I got sidetracked with my awakenings. Writing has its own introspection, even when that's not the subject. In my science fiction manuscript, I had a lot of trouble with my main character's backstory but not his foil. His foil is more like me, so it's been easy to

> write him. When I brainstorm about the main character, I always feel disconnected and slightly lost trying to create the needed depth. His foil? An untapped well!

My reply burst out of me without much thought. "It sounds like maybe your main character and foil need to switch places."

About a minute later, he wrote this:

> Such a simple answer staring me right in the face. I can't believe I never thought of that. I'm laughing out loud right now. It's like looking for your car keys while holding them. I'm going to try editing my manuscript with the characters swapped. Wow. That's going to fix it. Thank you.

The beauty of finding people who get us is that writers are about collaboration, not competition. There is enough space in this world for everyone to write. Writers inherently know this. Whatever we yearn to say, in whatever format we desire, we as writers lift each other up, and support and grow together. It is a special bond. We root for everyone and want everyone to succeed because it's not about winning or failing. It's about falling through this labyrinth of creation together and witnessing our imaginations out in the world. We don't want just our own words out there; we want to read others' words, too.

That's how it works.

Finding the right writer peers—people who support you, understand your journey, and inspire your growth—can be challenging, but it's also incredibly rewarding. It's easy to feel isolated in your creative work, especially when the writing process often involves long hours of introspection, self-doubt, and internal struggle to find your unique voice. The world of writing can sometimes feel unwelcoming, and it can be difficult to find peers who offer encouragement rather than judgment.

Think about starting small. Start with one or two trusted individuals who align with your values. Over time, you'll know when you've found the right people. Trust your instincts. If you feel genuinely supported, then those are your people. Focus also on quality instead of quantity. It's tempting to want to surround yourself with lots of writers, but a smaller, supportive circle often works wonders. Seek individuals who uplift your work, who are on similar journeys of growth, and who understand the emotional mountains we climb as writers. It's more about the depth of connection than the number of people involved.

Vulnerability is imperative to building your writing community. Writers often hesitate to share their work, fearing judgment. But opening up and sharing your raw work can foster genuine connections with people who can offer constructive feedback and emotional support. Be open to hearing other people's stories and challenges as well—it creates a sense of solidarity. Imagine then, that you are all falling together and how fun that could be.

Most importantly, building relationships that are worth your time, takes time. It's common to feel a little discouraged when it seems like everyone else has found their writing peeps. Keep showing up. The more you put yourself out there, the more likely you are to find your people.

Take time to create your community of writers. It may be one person, or one hundred people, whatever works for you.

Inspire, empower, support, encourage, band together. Focus on common aspirations. Help and share strengths. Dig into your weaker spots and learn from others. When you learn, share with someone who needs those insights as you did. Receive from your community and give back. As one of my writing mentors said, "Remember to send the elevator back down so others can rise up."

This leads me to the third C, which is Consciousness. Many wonderful books over the years have been written about consciousness. Philosophers, mystics, and scholars have analyzed, theorized, and excavated the depths of what it means to be conscious and how to raise our consciousness. A simple way to look at all this is from the viewpoint of awareness. Consciousness is about what we are aware of internally (within us) and externally (outside us). We can ask then, Where is our awareness? What are we conscious of?

As humans, we are always operating in this finite realm from a certain level of consciousness, with a certain level of awareness. The same goes for writers.

I was teaching a writing workshop that emphasized being more present in craft. One participant posed the following question: "How do we handle writing about real people in our lives, especially people who have wronged us or have done things that could be seen in a negative light?" A sensitive topic indeed.

The answer for me was something I had done in my writing: Write with love.

When we create anything with love in our hearts and with an intention of truth, we know we are doing the best we can, from the highest and most benevolent place. It can take some time to write like this, and it doesn't mean your words will be all puppies and rainbows. What it means is you have no mal-intent. You are writing as objectively and as full of love as you can. You will have communicated consciously, and the story will speak for itself. You need not add any negative energy behind it. If you have any, see if you can go back to your neutral place and work on what is coming up for you. Perhaps you need to revisit those fears and anxieties. By the time you write your story, if you can't write about this topic or person with love, go back and discover what is holding you back. These are relationships that could use some healing. If they were big, traumatic events, it may take some time to work through them. It's okay. Reach out for some support as you find your way to the other side. It's possible. I've done it many times and seen lots of other writers over the years do it, too. You've got this.

It may seem insurmountable. But it's not.

Cultivating higher consciousness as a writer is about shifting your awareness to a deeper level of understanding, both of yourself and of the world around you. It means writing from a place of authenticity, clarity, and empathy, using your craft not only to communicate with others but also to discover more about who you are and what you have to offer. The more you embrace this expanded awareness, the more your writing will reflect the richness and depth of the human experience. So, as you write, ask yourself, What am I truly aware of right now? How can this awareness enrich my writing? This deeper connection to consciousness will infuse your words with meaning and power, making your writing a transformative practice—not just for you but also for those who read it.

The most powerful example of consciousness in writing is one I witnessed this year. An elegantly dressed woman who walked with metal crutches approached me at a writers' conference about editing her collection of poetry. Since my one-on-one schedule was full, we set up a call to discuss her writing after the conference.

I didn't know anything about her poetry except that she was fond of rhyme, and it was based on her life's journey. On our call I asked her, "What's your collection about?"

There was a slight pause. Then, in a gentle and peaceful tone, she said, "I was sold as a child."

With just six words, my heart collapsed. Tears pricked my eyes. I thought maybe I had heard wrong. But I knew that wasn't the case.

She proceeded to share about her life and the poetic journey she was creating. How healing it had been for her to write about it all. And how she was ready to share the gratitude and grace and high levels of awareness gained from all the atrocities of her many years of abuse. Her poems were raw, honest, and vulnerable, taking the reader on a journey through her tremendous inner turmoil, to the insights she discovered, and to the freedom she has come to experience. Her book is a survivor's anthem and not at all written from a malicious place. It took her many iterations to get there. She confided in me that her earlier drafts of poetry were graphic and full of rage. Of course they were. She needed to write all that. But now, she is free and full of only love. Not for her abusers, no. For herself. For where she has been and where she resides now, in her peaceful, open heart.

If this woman can endure what she did and come to this beautiful realization with such serenity, then we all can. We can all raise our awareness, even if just a little bit. Yes, we need to feel our pain and heal from it, but then, the challenge comes to tell our stories from a different place. Not from a vindictive, anxious, or angry place. But from a place of knowing that what we are sharing—our story—does not define us, but has the ability to free us, and others.

Just as we raise our awareness, we can help raise the collective consciousness. Lennon's words demonstrate this point perfectly. From a world of separation, war, and disharmony, he took us to a higher level of awareness and consciousness—to peace and loving one another, without judgment, without dogma, and without limitations. He endeavored to do this in his own life and then shared it to uplift us.

When we take time to be aware and create from a higher place, a more conscious state, we become willing to step aside, letting the possible truths and beauty come through. Each step to a more neutral and loving place is a movement forward toward raising not only ourselves but also all beings on this planet.

Practice & Play

Your imagination is waiting for you. It can reveal what is deep inside you, yearning to come to life when you take time to dance with it. Take some time to get to know the captivating vastness that is your creative potential, and find new ways to keep it flowing. Play with all that arises and enjoy seeing where it all leads you. The following practices are integral for cultivating your imagination, and they can lead you to being more conscious and connected in a community of writers.

IMAGINE

Think back to when you were a child. What did you do that was creative? How did it feel? Why did you stop? What creative endeavors can you bring back into your life to enhance your creativity and to unleash your imagination? Often, it's not necessarily the exact activity that you long for, it's the feeling that activity or creative process brought forth. For example, I loved roller-skating on the Venice Beach Boardwalk where I grew up. For many reasons, I haven't roller-skated in years. But I can identify the feeling I had from it. It was the wind on my face, the feeling of freedom, the exhilaration of being out in the world and near the ocean. I now take fun dance-walks down the beach and gentle, enjoyable hikes. When I do, my imagination roams wildly, and it feels amazing. I gain creative insights and feel so free. What about you? What can you do to reignite your imagination?

BUDDY UP

There is nothing wrong with being alone. It's healthy to love ourselves enough to be comfortable being alone. I love being alone. I am alone right now. Okay, my cat is here on my desk, glaring at me as I type this, but you get my point. I also love people. And animals—yes, yes, my sweet cat. Here's the point. Writing is a journey that is meant to be shared. It is not a solo endeavor. Brainstorming is a perfect example. It's fun and electric, ideas being passed back and forth. As writers, we also often need other writers to help us see what we are unable to see. There are many more possibilities with two or more people reflecting on and exploring the same idea. Think about something you are unsure about as a writer or with your story. Be specific about what you need help with, then contact a writer friend and have a brainstorming session. Ask them to bring something they need some help with, too, so you can each have a turn talking through something together. Have them take notes while you share. Have them pay attention to what lights you up, to what isn't working, and to what needs attention or is confusing. Also, pay attention to what lights them up, to what they need and how you can be of service.

You can do this with someone who is not a writer as well. Just be prepared that the experience will be quite different since this other person may be an avid reader but not understand the mechanics behind writing. Practice brainstorming, and be creative with it. It is not only valuable but also super fun. There are no rules, only imaginations swirling and deeper connections being made. By buddying up, you are consciously creating connection and community.

If you don't have anyone to buddy up with, go out and find your people. Take the plunge and start making writing friends. Take writing classes and workshops, and attend writers' conferences. Go to author events and bookstores and libraries (yes, they still exist). Get out of that chair and meet people. And no, it doesn't count if you take your laptop out into the world and sit with your earbuds in and ignore all the people around you—or make them characters in your book. That is writing, not finding your peeps. Join a writers' group or create one of your own. It can take time to develop these relationships, so be patient. But once you find your people, oh my goodness, it is like being fully seen and heard and finally knowing your authentic you is understood.

RAISE YOUR CONSCIOUSNESS

Being aware and elevating our consciousness takes practice. When it comes to writing, we sometimes need to write what is burning inside us, to purge and release things. Not all of it is from our highest and best self. That's okay. This type of writing is important, giving us permission to get out everything wanting to be heard within us, the brightness and the darkness. When it comes to sharing our words, however, whether spoken or written, it is a different matter. How can we trust that what we are putting out into the world has a certain level of awareness? The answer lies in the practice of mindful reflection. Ask yourself, Am I coming from a place of clarity, understanding, and artistic expression? Or am I simply expressing unresolved emotions and thoughts without considering how they are received? What is my true purpose in writing this? What do I hope for readers to feel or understand from this? Ultimately, we are seeking to align our inner and outer worlds. Your words, when written from an elevated consciousness, will resonate more deeply, not just for you but for everyone who encounters them.

TELL THE TRUTH

When we tell the truth in writing, what we are really doing is making it believable, relatable, and intriguing. Readers identify with the truth and will know when something doesn't seem quite right. Whether in nonfiction (where it's imperative to tell the truth) or fiction (where it's fanciful and made up), your writing needs to be anchored in reality. Telling the truth will come most naturally when you write from your heart (not from your mind). The heart is where the truth of any story, character, or message resides. In essence, writing truthfully is writing with love. There are many ways to do this. Here are a few you can try:

- Take a piece of writing that is critical or harsh and rewrite it with a gentler and kinder tone, while preserving the truth of it.
- Review a piece for sensitivity. Ensure your words are considerate of others and their experiences. Think about how others may view your words. Hold respect for all beings in your heart, and allow your words to flow from this benevolent place.
- Be honest without blame. A story can be shared authentically without shaming or pointing fingers.
- Ensure a piece is balanced in both the positive and negative, without judgment for either. The events simply are, and there is a strength in writing from this neutral space.

Practice telling the truth, which, in all honesty, is a loving and transformative policy.

CHAPTER FOURTEEN

Be Transformed

Many of us think we want to read a book or watch a movie so we can distract ourselves and forget about our lives for a while. Perhaps that happens. But often, there is also something bigger going on, whether we are conscious of it or not. What I am referring to is transformation.

Writing is all about transformation. We know our characters are meant to change by the end of the story, and our audience will also change. We don't want to mindlessly absorb stories. Forms of art that leave an imprint, the ones we'll tell our friends and family about, are the stories that have sparked some form of transformation in us. Those are the gems. After experiencing them, we see differently, want to do something new, or change a part of our life. We are in resonance with a new energy or idea. We end up feeling things we couldn't have imagined without someone else's creative genius. We step outside ourselves for a little while, so we can go back in and discover ourselves.

That's what readers are looking for—to be transformed.

You as a writer will also transform. Yes. By the time you are finished writing whatever it is you are writing, you will have learned so much that if you started again, you would write your story differently—better. You will have stretched your mind and awakened your heart to a deeper calling, something bigger than you. If you don't feel changed at the end of a project, you weren't paying attention.

We human beings love beginnings—the newness and excitement of something about to start. What we rarely enjoy is being a beginner. We want to know things, to be accomplished, to be an expert. But with books and stories, jokes, movies, and plays and songs, we love not knowing what is going to come. We love being surprised and in awe of how it transforms. This can't happen if we aren't willing to be open and be a beginner. When we write, we need to exercise a beginner's mind. Let go of everything you think you know and start fresh. See where the wild ride for your new piece of writing is going to take you. Because, as much as we know, we really don't know much.

Each time we can show up with a beginner's mind, we make space for our imagination and, ultimately, for transformation. We don't know what is going to happen, but we know something will. Our ego steps aside, and we see our world, inside us and in our writing, with the freshest of eyes. We are not experts in anything. We are always learning. No matter how seasoned we are, there is always more to discover. Be with this, and celebrate moving up the rungs to more inspired and unexpected places.

As we progress through the writing process, it can often feel like the three-act structure. Act 1, the beginning, is incredible. We have an idea, a passion, and energy. It feels like a new relationship; we're inspired and in love. We see and feel only the positive. We can fly! Then, act 2 comes around. We are in the daily details of writing, and the newness has worn off. We are weary and unmotivated and want to get to the end. We trudge through, sometimes reluctantly, and many people give up. This is where the beauty lies, in remembering to be in a beginner's mind. Each time you show up to write, what can you see with new eyes? Be a beginner, all the time. Let something new come in.

We need to create new paths, which will help us enjoy what some refer to as the "sagging middle." It's the muddled midpoint of the story and the process. You may be focused on getting to the end. Remember how joyful the present can be. Make right now where you want to be.

Then, act 3—the ending. When you arrive, it feels amazing. You did it. You moved through so many aspects that needed attention, not only in the construction of your words but also inside you. You have transformed. You went on a huge journey. What did you feel along the way? Excited, empowered, afraid, or doubtful? Then maybe brave and persistent? Joyful and relieved? What did you learn?

Writing is perceived as a lone voyage, but it is a shared experience with a communal destination. Our paths may look and feel different with different terrain, but the results are similar for all: self-empowerment, self-acceptance, and self-love. We are all learning and growing as we write. What an incredible way to spend our time.

One beautiful example of transformation comes from a writer of contemporary and historical fiction. She was feeling stuck on the precipice, like something wonderful could happen with her writing but she couldn't see a way out, or rather, a way to embrace the fall. We had a long talk, and I asked her to complete an exercise. The inquiry was simple: What do you feel you need to let go of to make that leap? I didn't ask her what she thought she needed;

instead, I asked what she felt. I asked her to write a stream of consciousness answer and see what came up. A week later, this is what she shared with me:

> It's just words on a page. If I can remember that when I sit down to write, perhaps I wouldn't put so much pressure on myself.
>
> I have already learned to let go of so many things that have prevented me from writing: constructing the perfect sentence (every sentence), knowing all the minute details of historical aspects, having a flawless first draft. I feel confident moving forward knowing none of these are realistic or even attainable. And I'm perfectly okay with that.
>
> Unfortunately, what I am still holding onto is continuously feeding into my self-doubt. Knowing my "perfect" writing route. Knowing my hook, my genre. Wondering if everything should be outlined. Deliberating if I'm in over my head. Pondering if anyone out there would really want to read this story. Questioning if I'm "good enough." Making time for writing. Being able to write when I'm not in a good emotional headspace. Publishing options. A synopsis. A blurb. Doubting that I can truly finish

> this. Exposing my trauma to the world. These are what come to mind, but I'm sure there's more.
>
> When I first thought about writing my story, I just wanted to get it out. Even if it wasn't published, even if it was just for family, or just for me. When I received interest from an agent, that all changed. Suddenly, the pressure was immense. Now there's a possibility of being published. Now there's a timeline. I wonder if I can go back to the previous way of thinking while also keeping the offer in the back of my mind. That would be freeing.
>
> I would like to look at this story, not as something that *needs* to be written, but something that I have the honor of writing. I enjoy writing. I need to delight in the process.
>
> This is my proclamation that *I am* good enough. And, even if I'm not, that's okay, too. I am a writer because I write. All those doubts listed above don't matter. I just need to write. Because, after all, it's just words on a page.

Many things happened for this writer in this exercise. Her words capture the inner shift from fear and pressure to freedom and trust—a journey most of us writers have struggled with at least once. She also moved from her head to her heart. At first, she was mired in analysis, trying to figure everything out: the genre, the hook, the structure, the outcome. That's all mental. With the "letting go" exercise, she felt what she needed to let go. That pivot—moving from thinking to feeling—is where her transformation happened.

This writer was also willing to release her perfectionism. She acknowledged her humanity and realized striving for joy and creativity would be more rewarding. She made an affirmation that she is worthy, which is pure liberation. She was not waiting for anyone else's permission or validation. She claimed her space as a writer.

Lastly, she embodied trust. The phrase "It's just words on a page," carries so much wisdom. It's a return to the present moment. It's about the process, not the product. It honors the act of writing itself, without being overwhelmed or crushed by the outcome. It's the falling I've been talking about it. What a wonderful transformation.

Another writer I had the pleasure to work with was brilliant in so many ways: creative, intelligent, skilled with language, witty, and humble. I love her story, the way she has grown as a writer, and how she arrived at her final draft. In her words, this is a taste of her transformation:

> These pages began their life as a cookbook: a gluten-filled, sugar-laden, calorie-packed collection of my favorite dessert recipes. I envisioned sprinkling these tantalizing treats with some witty anecdotes from my life as a serial monogamist. Delicious desserts and disastrous dating—easy peasy, right?

> Well, that was the plan anyway. I never imagined the stories behind these recipes would lead me down a rocky road of unanticipated self-discovery.
>
> We give birth to our "children," nudging them toward the path we dream they'll travel, but, alas, our willful little darlings possess minds all their own. This book, like a mischievous two-year-old child, squirmed from my grasp early on, toddling off in its own direction, regardless of where I envisioned steering it … To ensure our offspring reach their full potential, we must accept them for who they are, not who we dreamed they'd become. This book knew it was a memoir at heart, yearning to escape, and I finally accepted that truth.

This woman is the epitome of a writer falling. Did she claw and fight her way through these pages? Yes, sometimes. But when she finally accepted her truth, what was yearning to be said, she experienced freedom. I believe she is a better writer and human for it. And whoever reads her book will have access to her deepest, most vulnerable truths and get to transform, too.

As you may have guessed from the examples throughout this book, I have had the absolute joy to meet, connect with, and work with so many fabulous writers. What a gift they all are to my life. They have all had transformations, some small, some huge. No matter the size, their inner shifts are always inspiring for me to witness. I learn from them, and I grow. That's one of the reasons I love what I do. And I love sharing these stories with you, hoping you can see the magic I see.

Writing can free you. Focus on that—on the joy and freedom that come from it. Whatever your journey is, whatever you are writing, it is worth your full attention, your dedication, and your beginner's mind. You can be transformed if you allow yourself to fall.

Write, let go, then write some more. Then see where the wind takes you. It is often a million miles away from where you thought you would be. And that can be beautiful.

Practice & Play

There are many ways in which words can transform us. Take time to explore new ways to be with your words and your process. Notice all the emotions and feelings around your creations. You are changing, growing, and learning through it all. Peer into those spaces and see what is there for you. It is often much more than you could have imagined.

ADOPT A BEGINNER'S MIND

Let's go back to the beginning, before you knew anything about writing except for the basics. Find that free space inside you that is willing to show up as someone new to the craft, new to your project, every day and in every moment. Pay attention to the freedom that you can get from this. What happens when you do show up with a fresh, new perspective? Pretend this is your first time doing something. Follow those new feelings and instincts. Bask in the joy of not knowing and discovering new aspects of your story, your writing, and yourself as a writer.

SHIFT YOUR MINDSET

We can change the world using creativity and ingenuity. Think out of the little box you may feel you're living in. Be fluid and opportunistic while keeping your guiding principles in mind. Adopt innovative approaches. Be willing to go somewhere new, somewhere uncharted. This doesn't mean you need to put pressure on yourself to adopt a whole new way of writing or create a new genre or type of poetry (although if you are inspired, please do). It can be as simple as a new way of doing things for *you*. What can you change? How can you see your piece differently? What about your mindset can you shift to create a new way of viewing what you are doing? Each time you write, take time to refresh your mindset, brainstorm, and find the thrill of discovering something new.

TRANSFORM

Take time to examine the books, movies, stories, poems, songs, and other art forms that have made a difference in your life. Pick one. How did the characters transform? How were you transformed after reading or watching? What elements of these transformations do you want to carry over into your writing? Why did they make such a big impact on you? By exploring the transformations that occurred, you will discover more truths about yourself and your why, and you will learn how to create a bigger impact in your writing. Repeat this practice with as many different stories and art forms as you like. Each time you can learn something new.

SAY FAREWELL

Sometimes what we write doesn't get shared. It might even end up in the trash. That's okay. But before you delete it, see if you can identify how it transformed you. What did you learn? How are you different for writing it and also for letting it go? If you have already deleted something, you can still do this exercise. Reflect on what the bigger purpose may have been for writing that piece. Did it propel you to your next piece? Did it free you from something? Did it heal you? Or maybe you don't know exactly what purpose it served, but you can tap into the emotions you felt from it. Whatever comes up may just be the reason you needed to write it. It was enough. In all cases, thank the experience and the words, and say farewell. But carry the lessons with you.

CHAPTER FIFTEEN

Be a Light

The cost of being a writer includes the possibility of what might never happen. There is an inherent risk with the unknown nature of creating something from nothing. Will it be worthy of our time? Will it be fruitful? Will it make any splash in the world? Lots of unanswered questions arise when we create from the mind. When we create from a place of lightness of heart and being, it becomes worth the risk because even if it is not what we intended, it can still be extraordinary. Something can always come from it. It just might not be the result we imagined.

Along the writing path, we get to discover what drives our story, what drives the reader to keep reading, and what drives us. We discover ourselves. If we are paying close attention, we'll get to see the bright light we emanate to the world.

When we have passion about something, we are in essence writing from our most inspired place. We open a hidden chamber where ideas and words are waiting to be released. We set them free to interact and play with them. Through our words, we are the light we want to see out in the world.

This is a gigantic privilege. We get to co-create our world.

Whatever we read and write becomes a part of us. In this way, words are like food. What we take in and what we create shape who we are. It also helps determine our level of consciousness. When we write, we are writing our future. We are writing what we want to see in the world, what we want people to engage with, talk about, and learn from. When we bring forth ideas, emotions, and thoughts into the world, we are choosing the light or dark that we wish to share. It's like one big potluck. What do you want your contribution to be?

There is nothing else like writing. We get to shed light on whatever it is we care most about, what is important, joyful, thrilling, and meaningful to us. If we want to reach people, we need to be willing to be bright, to come out from our hiding place. We need to let people see us and what we know, feel, think, and believe. Our lights can change the world—we get to decide for whom and how.

This may seem like a big ask. Shine our light. Change the world. In reality, it couldn't be simpler. Let's take literary master Kurt Vonnegut, author of *Slaughterhouse-Five* and *Cat's Cradle*. His writing may not be for everyone (as is the case for everything ever written), but he crafted stories that have made a lasting impression on millions of people. He shined his light brightly, and he didn't hide. One of the best pieces of advice I've ever heard from a writer was from him. He said, "Write to please just one person. If you open a window and make love to the world, so to speak, your story will get pneumonia."

Think of it this way: A genuine and deeply personal experience is more universal than something that is more general. By being vulnerable and writing for that one important person, readers will identify with it more and connect with the depth and true nature of what you are conveying. Write for one being, and your light will shine brightly.

Speaking of shining brightly, I am a big fan of Cirque du Soleil. What an inspired creation. From the intriguing stories, powerful music, elaborate other-worldly stage designs and costumes to the charisma and daring feats of the performers, it's an explosion of creativity and heart. I don't think I have ever experienced more light shining from one stage than from the last performance I saw called *Volta*—and I've seen almost every one of their tours (I did say I was a fan).

That night, I bought a program. I'm not normally a merch kind of girl, but this was too inspiring to pass up. On the front of the program in bold, gold letters was the theme of that show: "Find Your Free."

Yes, please.

What an incredibly simple yet profound string of words. As someone who plays with words day in and day out, I was amazed I had never come across these three words in this sequence. I am sure they were out there somewhere else, but to me this was new. And the light from them about knocked me over. The main character in the story was searching for his free.

Now, I could feel myself wanting to find mine.

After the show, I checked out the T-shirts, primarily because I wasn't ready to leave the big tent and the fantastic journey I had just taken. Then, across from me I saw it, a classic black V-neck shirt that had white letters strewn across. It said, "We rise by lifting each other."

The thrill of falling rushed over me. I recalled the performers gliding through the air and the feeling I had watching them. And then, those words opened me up. It felt exhilarating. Something in me shifted. I noticed how words have been a compass throughout my life, always leading me back to my truest self.

I grabbed the shirt, paid, of course, and have never forgotten the magic of that night. The performances were incredible, yes, but these two phrases have been guiding me ever since. Those writers expressed something I needed to hear.

Let a sense of buoyancy and lightness be the norm as you write. Even as you focus on productivity and impact, let the light of who you are be what guides you. Playfulness and a lightness of being can open you up to a creative and uplifting flow of energy. Be big-hearted and big-minded. Be the biggest you can be.

There are negative and limiting beliefs surrounding creativity, such as not feeling good enough. Don't believe them. Free yourself. Know that there is a lot more to creativity than you may realize. Use the power of your imagination. It's real. Imagination is the foundation of everything. Creativity is always happening. Be open to it. Give it energy. Feed it. Conceive it, and give it life. No holding back. Fall with all your heart.

And while you fall, shine and lift others up.

Shine and "find your free."

Practice & Play

If not another word was written, we could read each and every day for hours for the rest of our lives and never get close to reading a small fraction of all the words out there. So, do we need more books in the world? Absolutely! The world is constantly changing and growing, so we write more to match those transformations and new insights.

If you have a burning desire to share your words, there will be someone out there yearning to hear them. Shine for others to see. Be a light. Share what makes you come alive because inevitably that will bring other people to life. Here are some practices to help you shine.

LOOK FROM THE TOP DOWN

To shine your light onto the world, it helps to look at the whole process from the top down. Look at the biggest picture of your story/piece of writing you can imagine, the best-case scenario, the grandest idea, the highest level you could reach. Go there first. Go to the top! To the best feeling, the best reactions, the most intense and bright light. Once you have identified where you want to go, then come down, step-by-step to the details. How can you get there? What will help you reach that place? By starting at the top, you have removed any self-imposed limitations and boundaries, and you open yourself to seeing all that is possible. Then, from this vantage point, you can create.

INFUSE WITH LOVE

When engaged with a specific task or project, infuse it with love. Let that be foremost in your awareness. Transform your actions from mundane to sacred by visualizing how they will uplift another being. If your words elevate one being, they will assuredly uplift more. Practice infusing light and love into everything you create. See how this raises you up, and how it also raises others.

USE YOUR VOICE

Writing is the space between thoughts and ideas. The spirit of creating from the void, the dark matter among the stars. When we are in our most neutral and unattached place, this light comes forth. This is where you can tap into your natural rhythm of writing, your own melody. This is your voice and the flow you create. No one else has it and never will. This is your dance. Practice crafting strings of words and see how they feel. Listen to the voice that speaks from your heart. The one that shines brightest and feels the most expansive. This is where you'll find the *you* that wants to be seen, the part that will shimmer and bring forth your authentic magic into the world. Here are ways to help you with this practice:

- Start by putting together a few words or a phrase without overthinking it. Let your intuition guide you.
- If you have trouble writing, ask, What interests me most to write about? What feels natural and joyful?
- Identify your preferences by feeling what words, phrases, and themes you instinctively gravitate toward. Which ones lift you up?
- After you've written something, reread your words out loud. Pay attention to how the words felt when you wrote them, and how they feel when you say them. Take a moment to reflect. What emotions or memories come up for you?

- Make any modifications needed to your words, tightening for clarity and overall power of the message. Continue revising until you feel a sense of completion. This can take one or many revisions.
- Trust your inner voice. Let it guide you as you write, and help you to know when something you are writing is finished.

CONSIDER THE RIPPLE EFFECT

Books are not just products. They are energetic art pieces that bring connection and transformation. Think of your book/writing beyond the idea of a commodity. They have their own lives and energies. Consider the ripple effect of your writing. Where could your words lead? What could they do? What are the possibilities? What do you want to give to the world most? Knowing the answers to these inquiries can give you momentum and increase your passion and vision to create. It is also an important way to tap into your heart's yearning.

CHAPTER SIXTEEN

Be You

You have everything inside you to be a great writer. All you need to do is just be you.

You may be wondering why I didn't say this at the beginning of the book. It's because being you may be one of the more complicated endeavors you ever embark on.

Being who we really are isn't always easy. We get caught up in the world's frenetic pace and energy and ideas about how we are supposed to be, what is best for us and the world, and how things should be. We compare ourselves with others, judging ourselves and making changes that support a false idea of who we are. We become mired in confusion, going in and out of a blended sense of self.

We forget who we really are.

But we also forget we always have a choice—a choice to be ourselves, authentically and unabashedly.

Even when we are motivated and willing to discover our most authentic self, sometimes we don't know how. The *how* can feel impossible when we aren't clear on who we really are.

I spent a portion of my youth feeling lost—people pleasing, blending in, being a chameleon. Over the years, I have worked to dismantle these pesky little parts of myself as much as I can without judgment. Although most of the time I believe I'm as authentic as I can be, I still notice those sneaky aspects of the not-true me coming forward to fit in, to feel good enough, or to gain appreciation, acceptance, or love. We all want to be heard, understood, appreciated, and loved. We want to be a part of a community. We want to feel accepted for who we are, but often, in doing so, we change to meet the requirements of the world. Instead, we need to fulfill only one person's requirements: our own.

Think of your favorite writer, artist, or musician. How do you think they got where they are? Not by trying to fit in or by trying to stand out. But by going within.

They found within themselves what they were most inspired and passionate about and brought that to life. They did it because they couldn't imagine doing anything else. They had to create. It was the fuel for their masterpieces, an innate desire for expression—whatever form that was for them. The more they listened to their inner knowing and followed it to its full potential, the more authentic and brighter their light shined.

The talented musician Jason Mraz is a perfect example, who, by the way, is right up there with sea otters for me. He shared a story about writing his hit song "I'm Yours." He hadn't written in a while and was feeling disconnected from his artistry. He grabbed his guitar and started emoting, asking the universe to make him an instrument for whatever was waiting to come through, declaring, "I'm yours." He let go, opened up, and started singing, showing up, and being genuinely him. The song poured out in minutes, and he felt that deep connection to himself and his music. I always thought that song was about romantic love, but it's really about loving ourselves and daring to sing our song to the world. Mraz exemplifies authenticity and shines his light.

In the universe, there is only ever going to be one you. The exact molecules and genetic makeup, time being alive, and experiences you have been through, have created a one-of-a-kind expression only you can birth. You get this chance. Don't waste it trying to fit in and be someone else. Or pleasing a market, a genre, or an idea you aren't excited about or don't believe in. Be you. Be your own creation. When someone or something tries to disconnect you from that (including you), you are out of alignment.

Let go of what you think the world needs. Let go of what you believe the agents and publishers want. Even let go of what you believe the readers want, if only while you're in the flow of writing. Then, you can always step back into the revision process with ideas about how this can serve the highest good.

There is a difference between contributing to the world and following trends and ideas that don't feel authentic to who you are. It is a constant practice to get to know who we are and what we most want in this life.

Often there is pressure to be original. Let go of that. Focus on being authentic. It's all been done, so focus on what brings you joy. That is what will bring you the most fulfillment and help you shine the brightest light. At first, it may feel scary to be who you really are. That's okay. Often, our fears are imagined. Remember you're falling. It is really freeing once you get the hang of it.

When you write, don't just write. Notice the person you are when you are writing. Who are you? What do you want? What is happening? What is there for you to see? If you are scared, look closer. This is often where the magic happens.

It is that vulnerable place that holds so much beautiful artistic expression ready to be released.

Writing is a direct reflection of you. Writing has to be lived. You can't borrow someone else's truth. You can see how it has unfolded for one person when they completely let go of it, but you must make it yours. Practice reflecting about the words yearning to come out. Why are they important for you to express? Get to know the deeper reasons and the beauty of who you are and what you want to experience through your creative endeavors. The world is your stage. What do you most want to say?

How do we become our most authentic self? By simply being. When we force or try hard, we often push the very things we want away from us. I know, it's a little strange, but I didn't make up the rules. When you are being your best and brightest you, it won't feel like you're forcing something; you'll be too busy enjoying yourself to notice. Overthinking and stressing will take you away from this peaceful and creative place.

Here's the critical piece: Learn to be an exemplar of what your core message is, of what you yearn to share with the world. Detach from the world of convention, and connect with what is deep inside you. You are not the identities, labels, and words that someone places on you. You are not their thoughts, projections, or judgments. You are who you believe yourself to be. Do not be afraid to show *you* to the world.

There is only one right way to write—writing what feels true for you. Before we can write something for others to read, we first must write for ourselves. We need to know, love, and accept ourselves. Each of us is unique. We have our own purpose and expression in this world. Our voices and our messages are all different variations of human expression.

We need to follow what is true for us. Without this, we have nothing worth sharing.

I have been a part of the writing community for a long time. I've been a student and attendee, a newbie, a teacher and presenter, an editor and writing coach, and yes, a writer. I attend and work at writing groups, clubs, retreats, universities, conferences, and many stages around the world. In all these capacities, at the heart of it, I am a creative being who loves words. I show up because of my passion, and I share from that space. It is my fuel. It is my light. It is me.

I used to be a bit sheepish about my slant and philosophies about writing, the process, and the way I think about it and approach it. Over the years, I have become bolder and started to share my beliefs and ideas without excuses, without judging myself. The more I did this, the stronger my understanding became about who I was and how I wanted to be in this world. I learned more about what I could contribute and share. Before this, I worried people would not resonate with what I was saying.

The opposite happened.

The more I opened up, the more people I found who responded positively to what I was sharing. Most of these people had similar notions and were delighted I had expressed these ways of seeing writing and the creative process. My philosophy fuses writing and creative expression with spiritual concepts and ways of being. These together form the most authentic way for me to live. What has surprised me the most is that so many people who I previously believed wouldn't resonate with any of this, did. I made judgments and assumed others weren't thinking about, or wouldn't be open to, receiving my core expressions. I was wrong. And it's been so beautiful to see how wrong I was.

Not everyone wants to read or see what we create. But our art is not for them. It's for those who feel the energy behind what we have made. The people who do appreciate and recognize the value of our words are the people we are serving. And that's enough.

You can't learn to be you. You can only *reveal* you. Give yourself the gift of getting to know you again. You can learn techniques to write, but you can't learn the *you* factor. That is inside to be seen. To be embraced and shown. To be set free.

You have everything you need in you to write. Trust the big, beautiful being you are, and write from that authentic place burning inside you. That place that showcases the real you, the one the world desperately needs to see. Others are waiting to learn and grow from your experiences, from your brilliant, bright light.

Simply be you.

Practice & Play

There is a natural rhythm of writing, one that is yours and no one else's. This is the *you* who is ready to be seen. This is your tango with words. Unleash the wild and uninhibited you, and let it be free to create. Bring *you* into the world. No holding back. Follow these practices to a place of enjoying freedom of expression and discovering exactly who you are.

BE YOU

There is a place for *you* in this world. The *you* exactly as you are inside. The *you* that lives how you want to. To connect with this *you*, take some time to reflect on these inquiries. What comes up for you as you write to these? How do you feel? What do you notice? Be with your emotions and answers and see what you can discover about the real you that is asking to come to life.

- Why do I like to write?
- What do I want to write most?
- Am I being authentic when I write, or pleasing someone else?
- Am I writing as a finite being with a hidden intention, or am I writing from my highest and truest self?
- Will what I am saying add to the noise or improve the silence?

LOVE YOURSELF

Loving ourselves sounds simple enough, but it can be a lifelong pursuit. Like learning to do anything in this world, it can take time and practice. This venture is worth every bit of sacrifice. Practice finding ways to love yourself truly for who you are. Love yourself enough to know what you want to write. Love yourself enough to be excited about your creations. Each word you create from your most authentic place is an expression of self-love. If you are struggling with this, here are some affirming statements you can use to help get you there. Remember, affirmations are effective only when you speak from your heart and say them with conviction and belief. I like to say these while looking into my eyes in the mirror. It feels beautiful to love ourselves the way we love others. It only makes sense.

- I am shining bright for all the world to see.
- I am always free to create whatever my heart desires.
- I love and honor myself and all my creations.
- I love my ideas, and they are worthy of my time, effort, and energy.
- I have everything inside that I need to create.
- I love the process of bringing my expressions out into the world.
- I love myself.
- I am love.

WEAR YOUR PINK UNDERWEAR

I have this pair of pink underwear. It's comfortable and super cute. When I wear it, I feel like I have that extra something raising up my energy, something no one else knows about. I like to wear it when I do big speaking engagements or when I just need to remind myself that I am special—just like everyone else. What could you wear or hold or place on your desk or in your pocket that would give you that extra boost? Try to find something that can help shift your energy to focus on how wonderful you are, to remember that you have creative gifts to share with the world. No one else needs to know about your secret item but you. Except now, you all know about my pink underwear.

EMBRACE THE FINAL LETTING GO

There are so many things we've talked about in this book. A lot of them have to do with letting go of old ways, changing perspective, and adopting new ways of doing or seeing something. Letting go is an act of trust. Think of some things that you want to let go of—limiting beliefs, worries, fears. Are you ready to let go of one of them now? See if you can go there, push it over the edge, and watch it plummet far and away from you. How does that feel? You may have to do it more than once for things that are more difficult to release. Know this: The thing you need to let go of is a burden. It is causing resistance, slowing your magnificent fall. If you are not ready to let go of it yet, that's okay. Recognize it for what it is and how it is stunting you or keeping you back. Recognize that it is a burden. One day you will be ready to let it go. You will then get rid of the strain it has on you. And you will be free.

Go for it. Whatever it is.

It is waiting for you.

ONWARD

Here we are at the end. The cool thing about endings is they prompt beginnings.

It's time for you to move onward with your words, your insights, and your willingness to fall. But before you venture off the edge, I'd like to share one last thing.

We are all born with only two innate fears. Yes, only two. I'm not an expert in the field, but I feel like there are a lot more than two.

The first fear we all come into this world with is the fear of loud noises. At a primal, survival level, this makes sense since it is a reaction to a potential life-threatening moment.

The second innate fear is a fear of falling. Also known as basophobia, which is different from a fear of heights. Not everyone has a fear of heights. A fear of falling includes the anxiety from the sensation of falling, the feeling of being out of control, and the possible dangerous outcome of the fall. And falling, well, that goes back to what I've been saying all along, losing control.

Other common fears, like public speaking, snakes, failure, fear of looking silly, fear of not being liked, and fear of being judged, inherently feel dangerous … at least to our finite self. But writing? What's so scary about that?

I am not going to answer that. Not to be persnickety but because it doesn't align with my purpose for this whole experience with you. Instead, I want you to arrive at your own conclusions from everything I've said—your own truth. It's your fall. It's your time to find your free and all that comes along with it. I've had my experience with these words. Now, I give them to you.

Freedom begins the moment

you dare to fall.

APPRECIATION

This book is the culmination of quiet inspiration, frenzied typing sessions, uncomfortable moments of doubt, and steadfast support of those who believed in its possibility. As I jumped off the precipice into the unknown, there were many people whose presence, talent, and love were both a source of light and the heartbeat of these pages.

My deepest appreciation goes out to my wonderful writing community, to whom I owe my ever-growing passion to create. Thank you for guiding me toward my fullest potential and helping me become my best and brightest self. You are all dear to me, and without you, I'd undoubtedly be doing something else with my life—something far less fulfilling. Something like working as an undercover punctuation vigilante—secretly correcting signs and menus in the dead of the night.

Endless gratitude to those of you who generously took the time to read, edit, and provide valuable feedback on this book: Anna-Marie Abell, Julia Ballo, Leslie Ferguson, Marni Freedman, Beverly Hamowitz, Linda Kephart, Marijke McCandless, Reina Menashe, Adhara Mereles, Laura Perkins, Diane Rush, and Mary Vensel White. Your insights and suggestions made a profound difference. You helped shape not just these pages but also the soul between them—and for that, I am forever grateful.

My heartfelt thanks to all the writers whose stories have inspired me and whom I've had the honor of featuring in this book. Without you, this book would be a song half sung.

My most love and appreciation for the beautiful Asa Wild, whose artistic brilliance elevated the cover design and internal pages—thank you for continually bringing out the beauty in my words and in me.

To my wonderful family, friends, and my fabulous furry companion, Jade, thank you for loving me through this human journey and being there for me in both the darkness and the light. Because of you, I am living my dreams every day. What a fortunate woman I am to know and love you and walk this path together. Thank you for being with me as I continue to fall.

To you my dear reader: with so many beautiful offerings in this world, it means a great deal to me that you've chosen to spend your time with my words. I hope this book has offered you something meaningful for your life. You already have everything you need within you. All it takes is a willingness to go there. And remember, falling is freeing. I wish that for you.

ABOUT THE AUTHOR

Cherie Kephart is an award-winning author, writing facilitator, and developmental editor. Much of her work centers on helping writers discover their most authentic and creative voices. She is best known for her inspiring memoir, *A Few Minor Adjustments*, which chronicles her unforgettable journey with a mysterious illness contracted during her Peace Corps service in Zambia.

Her essays, short stories, and poems have appeared in numerous literary journals and more than twenty anthologies. A two-time winner of the San Diego Memoir Showcase, Cherie frequently presents at writers' conferences and retreats, where she is recognized for her empowering and compassionate approach to the writing process. Her other works include *The Healing 100* and *Poetry of Peace*.

When she isn't immersed in words, Cherie is likely dancing in her living room, wandering barefoot in nature, or hanging out with her ridiculously cute tortoiseshell cat, Jade. Cherie infuses her life and her writing with the same spirit of healing, creativity, and connection that guides her work with others.

Discover more at: CherieKephart.com

ALSO BY CHERIE KEPHART

A Few Minor Adjustments:
A Memoir of Healing

The Healing 100:
A Practical Guide to Transforming
Your Body, Mind, and Spirit

Poetry of Peace

STAY INVOLVED

Connect with Cherie on her Website

CherieKephart.com

Write a Review

for *The Upside of Falling*
on your favorite platform

Connect with Cherie on Social Media

@CherieKephartWriter

@CherieKephart

@Cherie.Kephart.Author

@Cherie Kephart

Made in the USA
Coppell, TX
13 June 2026

81421331R00132